THE STORY OF
TUTANKHAMUN

THE STORY OF
TUTANKHAMUN

An Intimate Life
of the Boy Who Became King

GARRY J. SHAW

YALE UNIVERSITY PRESS
NEW HAVEN AND LONDON

MIX
Paper | Supporting
responsible forestry
FSC® C106600

For information about this and other Yale University Press publications, please contact:
U.S. Office: sales.press@yale.edu   yalebooks.com
Europe Office: sales@yaleup.co.uk   yalebooks.co.uk

Set in Freight Text Pro by Tetragon, London
Printed in Slovenia by DZS-Grafik d.o.o.

Library of Congress Control Number: 2022942454

ISBN 978-0-300-26743-3

A catalogue record for this book is available from the British Library.

10 9 8 7 6 5 4 3 2 1

For Jack McKenna

Contents

Illustrations

Acknowledgements

I'd like to thank Heather McCallum, the managing director and publisher at Yale University Press London, for inviting me to write this book. It's wonderful to have had the chance to play my own part in the centenary celebrations – to delve into Tutankhamun's life and reconstruct his fascinating world. Her team at Yale University Press made this book possible, and I am grateful to all of them for their hard work and dedication. My thanks also go to the anonymous referees who suggested improvements to my initial proposal and the finished manuscript; to the book's amazing copyeditor Eve Leckey; to Heather Nathan and Kate Burvill for marketing and publicity; to Ken Griffin for his valuable help; and to my wife Julie Patenaude for reading and commenting on the evolving drafts of the manuscript.

Lille, France
May 2022

Introduction

1. The eyes of Tutankhamun's gold mask.

Tutankhamun. Unlike the names of many kings from the ancient world, Tutankhamun's has entered the public consciousness. People everywhere know the story of the discovery of his tomb; everyone has heard of the curse; everyone recognizes his famous gold mask.

But this should never have been the case.

Over three thousand years ago, the ancient Egyptians hacked out Tutankhamun's name from his monuments in a deliberate attempt to obliterate him from memory; his carvings and images were usurped by later kings, and he died young, before he could make a name for himself in Egypt and abroad. If things had gone according to plan, Tutankhamun wouldn't even be a footnote in history.

It is only the chance survival of his tomb, and especially the treasures within, that have brought the boy king to our modern day and made him a celebrity. But there's much more to Tutankhamun than just his treasures. Pieced together from clues left on his dazzling artefacts and other scattered monuments unearthed over the past century, his story is one of a short life, lived in interesting times.

THE BOY KING

Tutankhamun was born around 1329 BC, over a thousand years after sweating Egyptian workers heaved the Great Pyramid of Giza's last blocks into place, and about one thousand years before Cleopatra met her asp-poisoned fate locked in her Alexandrian tomb.[1] He grew up during a tumultuous era, when his father, King Akhenaten, had moved the royal court to a newly constructed city in the desert – modern Tell el-Amarna, ancient Akhetaten. With the famous Queen Nefertiti, this heretic king swept aside the old gods, attacked their images and names, and focused state worship on a single deity: the Aten, or sun disc. Later, when Tutankhamun came to power at the age of ten, his first job was to dismantle his father's movement and spearhead the return to Egypt's traditions. Urged on by his advisers, but acting in his own name, he restored and reopened ruined temples and re-carved smashed divine statues. As the years passed, Tutankhamun managed to re-establish order, a key traditional role of any Egyptian king, but this meant going against the life work and teachings of his immediate family.

It can't have been easy, and ultimately, he wouldn't even be recognized for his achievements.

After his early death, Tutankhamun's dynasty crumbled. His successors attacked his name and monuments, usurped his legacy, and a new royal line came to power. His tomb, hidden by flash flood debris soon after his burial, was quickly forgotten, and life continued as if the boy king had never existed. Little thought was given to him again until the first decade of the twentieth century, three thousand years later, when Egyptologists excavating in the Valley of the Kings unearthed a pit and a small chamber, each containing artefacts bearing Tutankhamun's name. These were thought to be all that remained of his burial – he was, after all, an inconsequential king.[2] But British archaeologist Howard Carter disagreed. Funded by Lord Carnarvon, Carter's search for the tomb began

2. Howard Carter looks into the face of Tutankhamun's second coffin.

in 1917 and, after years of frustration, succeeded in 1922. The 'wonderful things' Carter discovered made headlines around the world.

In an instant, Tutankhamun was back.

Since Carter's day, the tomb's treasures have toured the globe like rock stars, selling out exhibition halls everywhere, and each time generating a new wave of Tut-mania. Over the years, the boy king and his artefacts have inspired movies, novels, music, jewellery and architecture, while the 1920s media obsession with the tomb's supposed curse never dissipated. Documentaries too, often presenting new theories and research on the boy king's family or death, remain popular. In the twenty-first century, Tutankhamun's treasures have made their new home at the Grand Egyptian Museum, Giza, his mummy has been analysed using the latest scientific techniques, and studies of his tomb have raised the possibility of secret chambers lying hidden within. The treasures themselves have still not been fully examined by scholars, leaving many more revelations to come, and artefacts associated with Tutankhamun continue to emerge during excavations across Egypt, adding new details about his life.

Over three thousand years may have passed, but the story of Tutankhamun is still being written.

TELLING THE STORY

People today remain just as fascinated by Tutankhamun as they were when his tomb was discovered a century ago. Celebrity, royalty, riches, unexplained death, and a lost tomb, have proven to be an alluring, enduring, and intoxicating cocktail. When combined with the slow-drip reveal of fragments of information emerging from excavations or museum storerooms – the pieces of a puzzle, each bringing us one step closer – our interest is secured until the next revelation. And then the next. The developing story is a historical drama, police procedural, and soap opera rolled into one. There's always just enough new evidence to slightly clarify our understanding, but not enough to answer everything. It's frustrating – in a good way.

The arrival of the one-hundredth anniversary of his tomb's discovery presents the perfect opportunity to see what the accumulated mass of a century's evidence, interpretation, speculation, and argumentation has truly revealed about Tutankhamun's life and death. To build my reconstruction, I've studied the latest scholarship and prised out as much historical detail as possible from the limited surviving information. Where I've chosen one interpretation over others, to maintain the narrative flow I explain my reasoning and potential alternatives in an endnote,[3] and to keep a good pace, I only cover a period of about forty years in the fourteenth century BC, encompassing the time just before Tutankhamun, his reign, and the aftermath, before jumping forward in time to the twentieth and twenty-first centuries.

Objects from Tutankhamun's tomb, or those associated with him, illustrate events from his life, not just his death. A reed cut with his own hands from the marshes to help him walk. The wear on his sandals. Repairs to his chariot wheels. A lock of his grandmother's hair. These are not the tomb's flashiest crowd-pleasers, but these small details, and others like them, can help to add flesh to the bones of Tutankhamun's life, transforming him from a symbol of ancient Egypt into a human being. The artefacts also provide intriguing details about ancient Egyptian culture, such as kingship, court life, religious beliefs, and the afterlife, and let us explore Egypt's wider international affairs. In this way, Tutankhamun's tomb is a time capsule, providing a snapshot of life in 1300 BC – not just in Egypt, but across the Egyptians' known world.

My hope is that by the end of this book, you will see Tutankhamun in a new light. Not just as a remote and ancient god king, who died young and was buried with fabulous treasures; not just as a symbol or celebrity; but as a real person, with loved ones, personal beliefs, responsibilities, hobbies and health problems. A person who experienced a life of extreme luxury and personal tragedy, who felt the weight of re-stabilizing a country and continuing a centuries-old dynasty. A person who was almost eradicated from memory. A person who deserves to be more than just a gold death mask or a souvenir T-shirt.

Let me introduce you to Tutankhamun.

This book tells his story.

1

The Story of Tutankhaten

King Akhenaten sat beside Queen Nefertiti in the palace audience hall, each on a lion-legged throne, raised high on a dais above the people with gifts amassed below them. A gilded wooden canopy framed them, topped by two rows of rearing cobras – symbols of royal power, believed to spit fire at the enemies of order. The mood was good, and the royal couple held hands, breaking formality. Their six young daughters stood behind them, each sporting the long braid of plaited hair typically worn by children. While their parents watched the crowds assemble in the hall, they entertained themselves, smelling pomegranate fruits or playing with young gazelles, their royal pets. Among them was a princess named Ankhesenpaaten, the future wife of King Tutankhamun.

Akhenaten had been king for twelve years, and this grand celebration was the high point of his reign so far. His new city, Akhetaten, better known today as Amarna, had been under construction for the past seven years.[1] Finally, it was complete, and not only was it the new home of his family, but it was the centre of operations for his government too, replacing Egypt's other royal cities. People from all over the country had already moved to Amarna to start a new life. Today, he had the chance to introduce it to the rest of world.

3. King Akhenaten and Queen Nefertiti with three of their daughters.

On this grand day of celebration, while the royal princesses played, foreign delegations presented themselves before Egypt's king and queen, raising their arms in adoration and dropping to the floor to kiss the ground. The princesses watched as Nubians – people from the lands south of Egypt – stepped forward to offer leopards and antelopes, shields, gold rings, and blocks of precious metals, all carried in procession and placed on the audience hall's floor. The gold glinted in shafts of light cast from windows high up near the ceiling. Guards marched rows of prisoners of war, captured during a recent uprising against Egyptian control, their hands bound, feathers on their heads. Women and children walked among them. Some of the women carried babies in baskets strapped to their heads with bands. As the parade continued, men boxed and wrestled for the entertainment of the crowd. Guests chatted amongst themselves. Unfamiliar languages drifted through the air.

Next came the people of the Levant – vassal states of the pharaoh since the empire-building campaigns of Akhenaten's predecessors. They brought daggers, shields, chariots, animals, vases, and bound prisoners too – more unfortunates who would be sent to work in elite households and temple fields. Tribute also arrived from lands beyond Egypt's sphere of control. The people of Punt, a place far to the south of Egypt, brought incense. The people of Libya, tall feathers in their hair, came carrying ostrich eggs. The Minoans of Crete offered luxury items crafted from metal.[2]

When these foreign delegations arrived at Amarna, they saw an Egyptian city quite unlike any others they'd visited. The carvings of the king and queen appeared rather unflattering, showing them with spindly limbs and flabby bellies; the temples lacked their dark sanctuaries, and only one god was carved or painted on the temple and palace walls – a curious disc, high in the sky, its arms reaching downwards towards the royal family. Where was Osiris? Amun? Ptah? The gods they knew the Egyptians worshipped. Amun in particular seemed oddly absent, given his usual prominence. Wasn't he meant to be the king of the gods?

Akhenaten and Nefertiti knew the impact their unusual city, with its innovations in art, architecture, and religion, would have on visitors. Showing it off had been a great motivation for throwing the extravagant event unfolding before them.[3] Stories of their grand architecture and artistic vision and – most importantly – their newly elevated god, the Aten, or sun disc, would spread to kingdoms far across the world. Now that Egypt's traditional state god Amun had been put in his place – his temples closed, his priests sent away, his statues smashed – Egypt could have a new and brighter beginning.

And from the Aten's point of view as he crossed the clear blue sky above his holy city, Akhenaten had created a marvel. The god looked down upon a lengthy Royal Road that ran from north to south, parallel with the Nile. Designed primarily for royal parades, it was currently bustling with the chariots of dignitaries and servants, all making their way to the palace celebrations. The people of Amarna watched the spectacle from the sidelines, kept away by soldiers. Along the road's length, there were grand palaces, government offices, and huge temples, where hundreds of offering tables stood in the open air, piled high with gifts for the Aten's warm rays to touch. Smaller roads led eastwards from the Royal Road to the grand villas of Egypt's elite. Servants and the city's poor lived around these houses, while beyond on the city's desert fringes, workers quarried stone for their king, often malnourished, often dying young. To the east, in Amarna's lifeless hills, craftsmen cut and decorated tombs for the royal family and the elite, where after death, they would resurrect each day with the Aten.

The whole project was ambitious. Seven years earlier, none of this existed. Amarna had been a barren, empty space in the desert, lying just beyond the cultivated land on the Nile's east bank. Its swift construction was a testament to Akhenaten's devotion to his new god. This city would eternally be the Aten's cult centre and a home for Egypt's royal family, its chief worshippers. But absent from all this splendour and squalor, unseen and unmentioned in the monumental carvings and statues that commemorated the city's grand celebrations, was a three-year-old boy: Prince Tutankhaten – the future King Tutankhamun.

THE BIRTH OF A KING

When Tutankhamun was born in 1329 BC, much of Amarna remained under construction. While servants and workmen quarried stone blocks and moulded mud-bricks for the temples, palaces and administrative buildings, and courtiers pondered the best spots to sink their private wells in the grounds of their new villas, Tutankhamun's mother was giving birth in a pavilion erected in the grounds of Amarna's North Riverside Palace – the royal family's main residence.[4] She squatted, balancing, each foot on a mud brick to raise her from the ground, their sides decorated with protective imagery ensuring the safety of mother and child. Egypt's finest servants, midwives and doctors were at her call, armed with a mixture of ritual and magic to ease her pain and keep dangerous demons at bay.[5] In a time when child mortality was high, and pregnancy was dangerous for the mother too, the fact that both survived the birth was surely a blessing from the Aten. She called him Tutankhaten, the 'Living Image of the Aten' in the god's honour. The royal doctors examined the child and found him healthy, except for a clubfoot distorting the bones and ankle. They searched their medical papyri for cures for his condition, but without success. He would walk with a stick throughout his life.[6]

Tutankhamun's father was most probably Akhenaten, while his mother was one of Akhenaten's sisters.[7] She died violently between the age of twenty-five and thirty-five, when a heavy blow to the left side of her head fractured her skull – an injury from which she did not recover.[8] Details of her life, including her name, remain a mystery. How much time Tutankhamun spent with either parent, or where, is also unknown. As a baby, Tutankhamun's wet nurse was Maia,[9] a prominent woman in the royal harem.[10] Given their time together, Tutankhamun perhaps formed a close bond with her, and maybe even saw her as a second mother, especially if his own mother died early in his life. The children of elite Egyptians were often assigned wet nurses.[11] Princess Ankhesenpaaten – Tutankhamun's half-sister and future wife – had a royal nurse named Tia.[12] Queen Nefertiti had a wet nurse named Tiye, wife of Aye, a royal adviser to Akhenaten, his nephew.[13] Because of her proximity to the royal family, Tiye had the right to be represented throughout Aye's tomb, an honour infrequently given to wives.[14]

When Tutankhamun later became king, Maia would build a tomb for herself at Saqqara – a grand necropolis beside the great city of Memphis.[15] Within, artists painted Maia sitting on a chair wearing a long flowing wig, crowned with a blob of sweet-smelling wax – an adornment often shown worn by guests at banquets. Tutankhamun sits on her lap, presented as a miniature king wearing the helmet-like Blue Crown. Maia raises one hand to Tutankhamun's face, her palm facing him in a gesture of respect. A dog, perhaps a royal pet, is beneath her chair.

4. Tutankhamun and his wet nurse, Maia.

Given the closeness shown between nurse and child, it is possible that Tutankhamun himself authorized the painting – a reminder of the only parent he truly knew.

A ROYAL EDUCATION

Like any elite child, Tutankhamun owned a variety of toys. He played with an ivory monkey, whose arms he could move up and down,[16] and a small wooden bird.[17] He also had a fire stock and bow drill, which he could spin so the small bow created friction and heat, and ultimately, fire.[18] But from around age four, there was less time for play. He now spent much of his life learning to read and write, sitting cross-legged on the palace floor, a papyrus pulled tight across his legs. He first studied hieratic, a cursive form of ancient Egyptian used in daily life, before moving on to learn the sacred hieroglyphs inscribed on monuments.[19] Traditionally, scribes learned to write a classical form of Egypt's language, a version spoken many centuries earlier. But Akhenaten was anything but traditional. As part of his reforms, he commanded people to write in the language of his day, making Tutankhamun among the first to adopt this new style. Nonetheless, there were still standard texts that every student had to learn. After writing simple words and phrases over and over, and studying model letters to build his vocabulary, he copied ancient classics, such as *The Tale of Sinuhe*, about a courtier who fled to the Levant. His tutors must have been careful to omit any references to the traditional gods in their study texts, and particularly any mention of the hated Amun.[20]

There were wisdom texts to read too, particularly those that presented teachings passed from one king to the next – content that would have grabbed the young prince's attention.

Among these was *The Teachings for Merikare*, already centuries old by Tutankhamun's era. Set during a time of political breakdown, the pharaoh instructs his son on the weight of kingship, and gives wise advice on the importance of discussion over violence, respect for people and monuments, piety, and how officials should be appointed based on ability rather than status.[21] Composed during the same period, *The Teachings of Amenemhat* relate how the king, after being attacked, teaches the crown prince that no matter how well he ruled, there was always danger, even within the palace. To Amenemhat, kings had no place for trust.[22]

As a prince, Tutankhamun had access to the best scribal equipment in Egypt. He owned an elaborate wooden holder for the reed brushes he used as pens; inlaid with precious stones and gilded, it was designed to appear like a palm tree.[23] Any mistakes that he made when writing on papyrus were rubbed away with a handy piece of sandstone.[24] His scribal palettes were inscribed with his name, and had dedicated sections for his 'cakes' of black and red ink,[25] which he mixed with water. He used one of his ivory bowls so often that it became stained with red ink.[26] Given that red was often used for corrections, perhaps he made a lot of mistakes. Tutankhamun wasn't the only royal family member who learned to write. His half-sister Meketaten owned an ivory scribal palette, which had four spaces for pigment, filled with red, yellow and black colours. She was only a few years older than him, so they may have learned to write together. A palette owned by his oldest half-sister, Meritaten, had space for six colours, of which blue was her favourite.[27]

Princes were normally educated in the palace alongside other royals and select members of the elite, including the children of foreign rulers from regions under Egyptian control. The royal children also travelled to Egypt's provinces to learn from tutors outside the major cities. Sennedjem,[28] Tutankhamun's royal tutor, came from Akhmim, around 150 kilometres south of Amarna, so it was perhaps there that he gave the prince chariot riding lessons, improving his hunting skills and preparing him for a future as a war leader.[29] On these occasions, Tutankhamun wore child-size gloves, designed for charioteers,[30] and socks that kept his feet safe from the dust and stones thrown into the air.[31] He owned small bows,[32] and when shooting arrows, to save his left wrist from harm, he wore wrist-guards made from leather.[33] He also had a sling, which he used when hunting.[34]

Tutankhamun's other tutors would have been enlisted from the government administration. Given past precedent, treasurers, royal stewards, and even the vizier – the highest office in the land after the pharaoh – might have been called on to teach him.[35] From these assorted dignitaries, he would have learned management, geography, diplomacy, warfare, religion, court etiquette and morality. All of these skills would have been useful to Tutankhamun, for even if he never became king, princes were sometimes appointed to offices in the administration, military, or the priesthood.[36]

THE TEACHINGS OF AKHENATEN

Thanks to Akhenaten's religious reforms, the Aten was now Egypt's state god, and all other deities were to be ignored. In particular though, it was Amun, the Hidden One, who received his greatest scorn. Not only did Akhenaten change his name from Amenhotep, removing Amun, he ordered this god's images and names be hacked away from all monuments. With royal approval, the old ways were dead. In this new dawn, the teachings of Akhenaten were central. The Aten taught the king and he passed its words on to the people. According to him, the Aten was the creator of the world, of all people, of animals. When the god rose in the morning, he brought joy to all lands. People celebrated and the king made offerings to him. And when he set, the darkness brought dangers and a death-like state, which was only eradicated by the morning light and the rebirth it signified. The traditional gods had no role in this daily drama, to the extent that hieroglyphs spelling out the word 'gods' in the plural were made singular.[37] It's probable, then, that alongside Tutankhamun's traditional curriculum, in his earliest years of learning he received teachings directly or indirectly from his father.

While Tutankhamun studied and enjoyed his youth, either at Amarna or travelling around Egypt to visit tutors, destruction was never far away. For every beautiful new palace or villa he saw erected at Amarna, there was a temple to a traditional god falling to ruin somewhere else. Perhaps on his travels, he watched his father's followers taking chisels to images of the gods, disfiguring them beyond recognition or smashing away their faces; or he looked on as they scratched off the gods' sacred names from temple walls. Because Tutankhamun was educated in the modern ways of Akhenaten and the Aten, this must have all appeared very normal – expected even, given that the old ways were being swept away and replaced. After all, who needed Amun, or any of the old gods, when you had the Aten? Simultaneously though, when passing through the streets of Amarna on a chariot, or carried in his palanquin, he couldn't avoid seeing symbols of the old faith. People – even at Amarna – made no secret of wearing amulets to traditional deities and worshipping them in their homes. All the contradiction and confusion, the destruction and construction, must have left an imprint on the child prince.

Unless Tutankhamun's early tutors taught him about Egypt's traditional ways, his first experiences of temple worship would have been quite different from princes born before or after him. For centuries, Egypt's religious capital had been Thebes, centred on the massive temple to the god Amun at Karnak. Successive kings expanded the god's temple, lavishing gifts on Amun, his wife Mut, and their son, Khonsu, who were worshipped in dark, exclusive sanctuaries – places only accessible to the king and his highest priests. Amarna's temples – the temples Tutankhamun knew – were not like this. Akhenaten ordered his architects to reserve large rectangular spaces in his city for two temples dedicated to the Aten: the Great Temple to the Aten, and the Small Temple to the Aten. Huge stretches of this land were occupied by altars, where priests and the city's population left offerings to be seen and touched by the Aten as it passed over. Each morning, Akhenaten ascended great ramps to greet the god – worshipping it in the open air, immersed in its newborn light.

Akhenaten's new art style was also more familiar to the young Tutankhamun than traditional forms. In wall scenes and statuary, the king's arms and legs were shown spindly, and he had a round belly and large thighs.[38] Nefertiti was shown this way too, as were the princesses. Getting to grips with this new system was a challenge for Egypt's artisans, who had to practise to reproduce Akhenaten's vision. In his central Amarna workshop, the sculptor Thutmose used drawings and his own observations to create plaster heads of Akhenaten, Nefertiti and other members of the royal family. Thutmose's artisans consulted these master copies when sculpting statues, ensuring a level of quality and standardization. Copies could easily be made and sent out to artistic workshops elsewhere in Egypt too.[39] In this way, the new art could spread throughout the land, and eventually replace the artworks being destroyed. Thutmose's dedication to his craft brought rewards, in particular, a two-storey villa at Amarna set within its own walled enclosure. His plaster workshops stood next to the villa, and stones were carved by teams of sculptors in his open courtyard beside the compound's entrance gateway, through which the materials were delivered.[40] It was there, in his villa, that he kept his master copies, including the famous bust of Nefertiti. Though it's unlikely that Tutankhamun ever visited Thutmose's home, he would almost certainly have seen its creations.

5. A statue of King Akhenaten, displaying the unusual art style of his reign.

PLAGUE AND DEATH

Under cover of darkness, a black flea leapt from bed to bed in a house within the Workmen's Village at Amarna. Whenever it landed on its sleeping human host, it sucked up a pleasant gulp of blood before moving on to the next meal. With each bite, it gave something in return: deadly bacteria. The village was self-contained, standing just west of the royal tomb, away from the main city. Within its rectangular walls, there were seventy-two small houses, arranged in six rows along straight streets, where the royal artisans and their families lived.[41] Fleas were a frequent annoyance in the village – there's nothing like trying to carve or paint a beautiful scene whilst having to scratch an irritating itch. But as the artisans fidgeted and cursed during their days in the tombs, they could not have known that these same fleas were spreading bubonic plague.[42] Across the village, families watched helplessly as their loved ones, friends and co-workers developed fevers. When the fever worsened, their lymph nodes swelled and became painful and black. They suffered from chills. They grew weaker. Little could be done for them and the end result was usually the same: death, followed by burial in the village's cemetery.

The Workmen's Village at Amarna was a microcosm of wider suffering. Plague was already rampant in other parts of the eastern Mediterranean world. The king of Cyprus had sent Akhenaten a letter explaining how his copper mines were being underexploited because many of his workers had died from a plague. This same disease had swept through the island's population and killed members of the royal family.[43] Akhenaten received letters about the plague from the king of Babylon and the rulers of the Levantine cities of Megiddo and Byblos too. The latter mentioned news of the plague in Sumur.[44] Was Akhenaten's grand international get-together at Amarna – the highlight of his twelfth year as king – a major 'superspreader' event?[45] Had the plague left from Egypt or arrived in Egypt? Whatever the case, only two years later, tragedy struck at the heart of Akhenaten's empire.

During the fourteenth year of Akhenaten's reign, Princess Meketaten, the second oldest of Akhenaten and Nefertiti's daughters, died. She was around ten years old. Whether her death was caused by bubonic plague or another disease, remains unknown. With no place to bury her, the grief-stricken royal family sent artisans to cut and decorate a suitable chamber in the royal tomb under construction in Amarna's eastern hills. To eternalize their grief, they asked artists to carve an image of Meketaten's body lying on a funerary bed, surrounded by mourners, including Akhenaten and Nefertiti. One woman, turning away from the body, stands nursing one of Nefertiti's babies, probably representing Meketaten reborn.[46] In that dark chamber, the Amarna royal couple laid their daughter to rest in a small granite sarcophagus.

At around this same time,[47] the two youngest princesses, Neferneferure and Setepenre, also died, and were buried in a chamber beside Meketaten's in the royal tomb. They were followed soon after by Queen Tiye, Tutankhamun's grandmother. The sarcophagus containing her body was surrounded by a gilded wooden shrine in Akhenaten's own burial chamber – a sign of the king's deep affection for his mother. The artisans once again set to work crafting a scene of the royal family in mourning[48] – one that, sadly, they had gained much experience carving. To add to the family's loss, Queen Kiya, one of Akhenaten's secondary wives, also died. Her monuments were usurped by Princess Meritaten. For all its celebration of new life – an Egypt reborn – death had become a constant companion in Akhenaten's city.

Painfully aware of the danger to his family line – and by extension, to the survival of his dramatic reforms – Akhenaten appointed an obscure royal family member named Smenkhkare as his co-regent.[49] Smenkhkare married Princess Meritaten – probably only thirteen years old at this point[50] – and they started appearing together in official life. Among their duties, they presided over a reward ceremony for the harem official Meryre II, who served Nefertiti. As this was a ceremonial role that normally fell to Akhenaten and Nefertiti, it showed the assembled nobles who the king expected to succeed him. Smenkhkare also presided over the construction of a grand columned hall within Amarna's Great Palace, but he wouldn't have long to enjoy it. After only two years as co-regent, he too was dead, throwing the succession into turmoil once again. By this point, surely even the royal family had doubts about Akhenaten's religious reforms – were the traditional gods angry?

Then, in 1321 BC, after seventeen years on the throne, Akhenaten died. Servants sealed the palace gates in a gesture of respect. The royal court went into mourning. Everyone wondered what the future would bring. Soon after, the king was buried in the royal tomb at Amarna, rejoining his mother and daughters. Artisans carved images of Nefertiti at the corners of his sarcophagus, in place of the four traditional goddesses, and his shabtis – magical figurines meant to serve the dead in the afterlife realm – lacked the texts of traditional spells believed to animate them. It appears, then, that Akhenaten had no deathbed recantation of his beliefs. Tutankhamun was around eight years old at this time, and surely attended the royal funeral. Due to his youth, he was probably unaware that not only had he experienced the death of his father, but of Akhenaten's reforms too.

The world in which the prince had grown up and accepted as normal was about to change.

THE REIGN OF KING NEFERNEFERUATEN

Over the course of half a decade, the royal family had been entirely decimated and now Akhenaten's vision was in jeopardy too. Luckily, there was an obvious successor to continue developing the new Amarna religion: Queen Nefertiti, who ascended the throne as the female King Neferneferuaten.[51]

6. The bust of Queen Nefertiti, discovered at Tell el-Amarna. The queen ruled as King Neferneferuaten.

Both she and Akhenaten were the driving force behind every change that Egypt had experienced over recent years. She had accompanied the king during lavish ceremonies and served as a priestess in the temples of Aten, to the extent that certain monuments exclusively showed her and the princesses making offerings. But now, even as the sole remaining torch-bearer for their reforms, she must have understood that there had to be compromise. Akhenaten had attempted to wipe the cult of Amun from existence, but there were many people across Egypt who felt uneasy about this eradication of tradition. Neferneferuaten addressed these concerns by doing something Akhenaten would never have considered: she allowed the cult of Amun to return and exist alongside the new Aten-centric religion.

As part of her compromise, Neferneferuaten accepted that kings would not be buried at Amarna. Some traditions were worth keeping, so she abandoned construction of her Amarna tomb, and planned a new burial site at Thebes in the Valley of the Kings, along with a mortuary temple in the plains below the valley, where her soul could be worshipped and receive offerings.[52] Artisans began crafting treasures for her burial,[53] objects that, like her own reign, would reflect a mixture of Amarna art and tradition. She asked that a sarcophagus be carved of red quartzite, with the traditional goddesses at its corners, each standing with outstretched arms. The sculptors were a little uncertain of how to execute the traditional design, and ended up carving some figures with a definite Amarna flavour.[54] They also crafted gold bands to be placed around Neferneferuaten's body when she died, four small coffins to hold her mummified internal organs, and a pectoral decorated with the goddess Nut[55] – one of the traditional gods of Heliopolis, who represented the sky.

Perhaps their greatest effort, however, was spent on crafting her gold death mask.

THE GOLD MASK

Neferneferuaten's eyes were drawn to the blue and gold striped headdress. Above a golden representation of her face, at the brow, were a vulture and a cobra, symbols of rule. On her chin was a long false beard, connecting her with the divine. Around her neck was a broad collar of precious stones. When inspecting the gold death mask that she expected to wear for eternity, Neferneferuaten must have been impressed with the quality of its craftsmanship, its beauty, its elegance. But she probably didn't dwell too much on the hands that its precious materials had passed through to reach that moment.[56]

The mask's copious amounts of gold – in mythology, the 'skin' of the gods and a symbol of everlastingness – had been brought from Egypt's Eastern Desert or Nubia. Toiling in the dry river beds of these gold-rich regions, people gathered sand from the ground, mixed it with water in pans, and swirled the contents until the water overflowed. If they were lucky, chunks of gold were left behind. Others – men, women and children – collected quartzite containing veins of gold from the ground or used chisels to hack pieces from rock faces. They smashed these quartzite chunks into fragments and ground them with a pestle to release the tiny bits of gold from within. Then they washed the stone fragments in a pan to ensure that no gold was lost. The gold was collected, melted down and moulded into ingots,[57] which were weighed, recorded and despatched.

The finest gold, piled high on a boat, made its way to the royal storehouses where some was selected to make

Neferneferuaten's death mask. In the royal workshop, the artisans beat the gold into shape, crafting its component pieces separately, among them the face, ears, headdress and back section. Crafting the face, they glanced at a copy of the king's official portrait created from a mould, the original of which was kept by the master artisan.[58] When the sections were complete, the artisans fitted them together so that the mask appeared as one seamless masterpiece, the rivets and solder marks rendered invisible.[59]

To complete the gold mask, the artisans selected other materials from the royal stores. For the eyebrows and make-up around the eyes, they shaped lumps of lapis lazuli.[60] These had started life 330 metres up a mountainside in Badakhshan, Afghanistan, in mines only accessible for three months each year. To free the lapis lazuli from the rock face, miners laid wood against the rock and set it alight. Slowly, the rock heated up, and when the moment was right, they poured water over it, breaking its surface enough to let them hack away chunks of the precious material. From the mines, traders took the lapis lazuli to Babylonia, either by land routes or by sea. It was then sent to Egypt as a gift of the Babylonian king to the pharaohs, travelling via the port city of Byblos in Lebanon for the sea route, or overland across Sinai. Some of Egypt's lapis lazuli supply was taken as spoils of war in the Levant.[61]

For the mask's broad collar, among the precious stones selected was turquoise, extracted from mines in Sinai, amazonite from the Eastern Desert, and carnelian, found in the desert areas to Egypt's east and west.[62] To form the white of the eyes, the workmen mixed magnesite powder and glue, and for the pupils, they used obsidian,[63] perhaps brought from Ethiopia.[64] For the blue stripes of the headdress, the artisans inlaid a form of blue glass.[65] Finally, with the addition of the cobra and vulture at its brow, and the divine beard on the chin, the mask was complete, ready to be worn for eternity.

THE DEATH OF NEFERTITI

There was tension at court. For those who wanted it, tradition was returning, but the cult of the Aten remained active at Amarna.[66] Neferneferuaten had not fully broken with Akhenaten's teachings, so Egypt was torn between the old ways and the new. Although the king planned on being buried at Thebes, her main residence was still at Amarna, where artisans had painted her name as king on the walls of the North Riverside Palace,[67] once her home with Akhenaten. Neferneferuaten's message was clear: she wouldn't be going anywhere soon. To her, Amarna had a grand future ahead of it as the focal point of royal life and ceremony. The traditional centres of Thebes and Memphis would remain secondary. The charioteer Ranefer clearly felt the same way. He chose this moment to renovate his Amarna villa, and as a sign of his dedication to the royal family, had Neferneferuaten's name written on his front door.[68]

But Neferneferuaten only reigned for three years, just long enough for Akhenaten's reforms to be relaxed. The events surrounding her death are lost. She never received a king's burial and her beautiful funerary goods were left to gather dust in storage.

Before the age of ten, Tutankhamun had experienced tragedy after tragedy. Among the dead were his parents, his grandmother, three half-sisters, Smenkhkare and Queen Kiya. Queen Nefertiti could now be added to this long list. It must have been a confusing time for the prince, about to be crowned king. Although still young, he was old enough to have absorbed Akhenaten's teachings and his aggressive dismissal of the traditional gods. Now, the old ways were returning, and two systems coexisted. Amun was back. All the turmoil – the closed temples, the mutilated artworks, the suffering and deaths of the people who built Amarna – was, in the end, for nothing.

2

Restoring Order

The ten-year-old king sat on a child-size throne, surrounded by the opulence of his palace audience hall in Memphis. In his hands, he nervously gripped the symbols of his rule, a crook and a flail, similarly child-size.[1] Over his wig, he wore a headdress of yellow and blue striped linen. A diadem was wrapped around his forehead, with a vulture and cobra jutting out at the front, dominating the top of his eyeline.[2] On his chin was a long false beard, tied with metal loops around his ears to secure it in place. He wore the finest white linen, pleated at the shoulders in the fashion of the day. A pectoral with a vulture hung around his neck.[3] He placed his feet, slipped within leather sandals, on a foot rest decorated with Egypt's enemies. His gilded throne stood at the centre of a large wooden kiosk, raised on a dais reached by steps. Its size made the king and his throne appear even smaller. From his lonely vantage point, the king stared down at the men arranged below him; a servant at the entrance to the audience hall had placed them in two rows according to rank, and told them to remain silent. They were much older than him. He recognized many of them from his father's reign. Now, they raised their arms in adoration to him.

Tutankhamun's eyes scanned the room as each courtier stepped forward in turn to lie on the floor and kiss the ground. The floor was painted with scenes from nature – pools filled with fish and birds in the marshes. Morning light falling from windows illuminated carvings on columns of his royal ancestors smiting Egypt's enemies. The name of King Tuthmosis I, builder of the palace, was painted in bright hieroglyphs. Following the instruction of his tutors, Tutankhamun asked the vizier about the business of the day – how was Egypt doing? The vizier stepped forward to report. The restoration of the old cults was progressing as planned – the gods would be pleased. The king nodded. The newly appointed Viceroy of Kush had settled into his position in Nubia, and there were no signs of rebellion in this southern territory. On a less positive note, the

7. Tutankhamun's diadem, discovered on his mummy.

Hittites were causing trouble on the north-eastern fringes of the empire. Unfortunately, the city of Qadesh remained under their control. Tutankhamun vaguely remembered his father talking about these problems. The courtiers listened attentively to the exchange, and then voiced their own thoughts and opinions on the matters of the day, taking care to get to the point and speak with respect for rank. When the king spoke, everyone listened.[4]

Despite their respectful behaviour in the audience hall, each of these men had their own plans, expectations, and hopes of influencing the young king. Born of elite families, who sometimes created mini-dynasties of their own by passing their offices to their children, they oversaw the major branches of Egypt's state: the government, the palace administration,

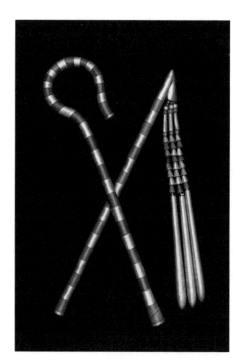

8. Tutankhamun's crook and flail, symbols of rule.

9. This vulture pectoral, found in Tutankhamun's
tomb, shows signs that the king wore it in life.

the priesthood and the military. But no matter how much
power they accrued, each answered to the pharaoh. With
Nefertiti dead, whoever had the child king's ear would be
the most powerful courtier of all, capable of creating great
opportunities and benefits for their families. The reality was
that General Horemheb, the highest military official in the
land, now had oversight of every government office. Aye was
senior adviser to the king, and a rare surviving member of
the extended royal family. And a man named Maya was in
charge of the treasury, consequently controlling all of the
kingdom's assets. Each of these men had direct access to the
young king who, despite his prominence in ceremony and
ritual, was still being educated – now more emphatically in
the traditional ways.

Once the audience ended, Tutankhamun took his walking stick and stepped down from his throne. He turned to the back of the audience hall, and slowly passed through a door into his private chambers. Once the Son of Re had set like the evening sun, the assembled courtiers filed out of the hall, passed through the large columned hall beyond, and then out of the palace into the late morning sun. Beyond the palace enclosure walls, the city of Memphis stretched off in all directions. Tutankhamun – still Tutankhaten early in his reign – had to quickly grow used to presiding over such formal audiences. When younger, he'd watched similar events, absorbing the rules and etiquette, and now he had to oversee crucial government meetings each morning as his first duty of the day. For a child who had spent much of his life with tutors or other palace children, kept out of the limelight, it was a drastic change. His courtiers managed much of the detail, but decrees were issued in his name, and convention dictated that only he could announce important decisions, sometimes in front of large gatherings.

But there was more.

Egypt's well-being, and that of the cosmos itself, relied on Tutankhamun to perform rituals correctly. He had to say the right words and make the right gestures at the right times. Failure could spell disaster. As he well knew, the king was responsible for divine order – a concept that the Egyptians called maat. Since his coronation, he had become the intermediary between the people and the gods. Given recent events under his father, he needed to make great efforts to regain divine favour. His performance as a priest, then, was just as important as his performance as a leader in the audience hall. And like every pharaoh of his day, he had to promote himself as a warrior too, defeating Egypt's enemies at the front of his army. His artisans immortalized each of these roles in art. His image, absent from temple and tomb walls as a prince, was now painted and carved across Egypt's empire. Statues, whether of himself or the gods, bore an idealized version of his face.

He may still have been a boy, but the fate of the world rested on Tutankhamun's shoulders.

TUTANKHAMUN'S CORONATION

To perform the many duties of a pharaoh, Tutankhamun had begun his reign by undergoing the coronation ceremony, an event that enabled the royal ka to inhabit his body.[5] Although everyone had a ka spirit – it was a form of life-force or double formed by the gods at the time of a person's creation – the royal ka transformed Tutankhamun from a normal boy into a god king. This divine spark was limited by the physical form and human failings – its host could get sick, make mistakes and even die – but remained, nonetheless, a powerful force. As a result, the Egyptians placed the king in his own category of being, somewhere between humans and true gods. This is why Tutankhamun was referred to as a 'good god' – a royal epithet – rather than a 'great god' like the divinities Re, Osiris and Isis.[6]

On the day of his coronation, Tutankhamun wore a cere-monial tunic, decorated with beads of blue and green glass laid out in diamond shapes, and gold sequins.[7] As the ceremony commenced, priests of Egypt's traditional gods, representing the four cardinal points and the limits of royal control, poured water over Tutankhamun's head, transferring the power of these directions into his body, and anointed him with oils. Then, with a crook of power hooked around his arm, he suckled the god-dess Isis in the presence of Min-Amun-Re, a god symbolizing fertility, the hidden and the light. Like a newborn god with his divine mother and father, Tutankhamun began his life again. He then recited lists of offerings before the gods, in particular the Theban triad of Amun, Mut and Khonsu. His words magically manifested these items for the divine.

Next, priests carried Tutankhamun on a palanquin to shrines that represented Egypt's north and south. In each shrine, he knelt, facing a priestess playing the goddess Mut, who held a symbol of life to his mouth from the end of a staff. Behind him, a priest acted the part of different gods, uttering words of power as he placed a succession of crowns upon Tutankhamun's head. Among these gods were Horus, Seth and Amun, the enemy of his father. Amun placed the Blue Crown – a large helmet – on Tutankhamun's head. Royal artisans later immortalized this event by carving a statue of the god gently touching the back of the Blue Crown worn by the kneeling king.[8] Later, a god lowered the blue and yellow striped nemes headdress onto the king's head. It was topped with an elaborate array of rearing cobras, papyrus bundles, falcons and horns – a form of crown popular under his father.

Once crowned, the priests handed Tutankhamun his child-size crook and flail, which symbolized his power. The god Thoth declared him king and his staff sent letters to government offices across Egypt, announcing the four extra royal names that Tutankhamun had chosen to be written in all official royal business alongside his birth name. Tutankhamun then fired arrows to the cardinal points, offered to his ancestors, and ate a piece of bread baked in the shape of the hieroglyph signifying 'office'. He showed his dominion over Egypt by symbolically circling the country, perhaps by following a path around a temple or shrine. Once the festivities were over, the royal artisans crafted a ceremonial corslet, its collar of semi-precious stones attached via a pendant and straps to its lower half, which wrapped around the belly and resembled feathers. The pendant bore an image of Amun crowning the king in the presence of the goddess Iusaas and the creator god Atum.[9]

QUEEN ANKHESENAMUN

At the coronation, and through all the events of his reign, Tutankhamun was accompanied by his wife and half-sister, Ankhesenamun. Like Tutankhamun, Ankhesenamun had changed her name when tradition returned – hers from Ankhesenpaaten, with the Aten ejected in favour of Amun. At the time of Tutankhamun's coronation, she was only eleven years old,[10] and Tutankhamun a year younger at ten. The two were already married, making Ankhesenamun Egypt's queen. Even in ancient Egypt, this was a young age for a marriage, but it was important for a king to have a Great Royal Wife to embody

10. A scene from one of Tutankhamun's thrones, showing the seated king with his wife, Queen Ankhesenamun.

35

the female side of kingship. There was no formal wedding ceremony or contract in Tutankhamun's time; it was enough for Ankhesenamun and Tutankhamun to share a home, their property and income. Though pharaohs usually had a single Great Royal Wife, they could have multiple secondary wives and a harem. Tutankhamun was no different. A woman named Taemwadjsi oversaw his harem,[11] though Ankhesenamun is the only queen mentioned on his monuments.

Powerful queens were not unusual in Ankhesenamun's family. Her mother, Nefertiti, had ruled as king, and even beforehand, had presented herself as smiting Egypt's enemies, a traditional prerogative of the pharaoh. It had only been 150 years since another queen, Hatshepsut, had become king, ruling alongside the child king Tuthmosis III; and even before her, the great deeds of Queen Ahhotep I were carved onto a stele erected by King Ahmose I, proclaiming her military achievements during a time of great danger for Egypt.[12] Ankhesenamun learned about these great queens as a child, watched the role played by her mother, and had witnessed more dramatic events than many do in a lifetime. Over the years, she had been present at Akhenaten's great international gathering at Amarna, had supported her mother when performing rituals to the Aten in Amarna's temples, and had watched a city rise from an empty desert. She had mourned the loss of her sisters, grandmother and parents and lived through the Aten's downfall and the return of Amun. By the age of eleven, she was already more qualified than anyone to be Egypt's queen.

In this role, Ankhesenamun accompanied Tutankhamun during royal audiences and reward ceremonies,[13] and exchanged letters with foreign rulers, demonstrating her political influence both at home and abroad.[14] She also owned estates,

managed by her own staff.[15] But her most important responsibility was ritual. Although the king and his priests took
centre stage in the temples, the queen represented Egypt's
goddesses, a role that was emphasized through her crowns.
When she stood behind the king, shaking sistra[16] – musical
instruments – and making offerings,[17] she wore cow horns as
a symbol of Hathor, a sun disc and feathered plumes.[18] On
other occasions, she wore a crown of double rearing cobras
symbolizing the goddesses of Upper and Lower Egypt, or a
vulture headdress with a rearing cobra.[19] These crowns were
conduits of divine power, which passed through her into the
world of mortals.

As the years passed, Tutankhamun and Ankhesenamun
tried to have children. Sadly, one pregnancy ended after five or
six months, and the other child was born at nine months, but
died soon after. Both baby girls were mummified by the royal
embalmers.[20] For the royal couple, these deaths were not only
personal tragedies, but reminders of the family deaths they had
experienced at Amarna and the weight of the need to keep the
royal dynasty alive.

THE RESTORATION BEGINS

Shortly after his coronation, Tutankhamun, led by his courtiers,
set in motion efforts to undo Akhenaten's religious reforms.
Neferneferuaten's coexistence between the Aten and Amun
was to be scrapped: the Aten had to go. To celebrate this new
beginning, the king asked his scribes to compose a text that
would be sent out across the country and carved on stone stelae
in prominent positions at temples.[21] These could be copied
by local scribes and disseminated, or read out to crowds on
special occasions, such as festivals. The text painted a drab

picture of Egypt before Tutankhamun. The gods had abandoned Egypt. They didn't care when people called for them.
The temples had been neglected, fallen apart, and become
overgrown. Egypt's armies failed on their missions when sent
out to fight abroad. Luckily for Egypt, Tutankhamun now sat
on the throne and everything had changed. It didn't matter
that undoing these events had yet to take place – the text was
composed too early in the young king's reign for anything to
have happened – just by writing them down they magically
became reality. This was the power of the written word and
how Egyptian magic worked.

Making such a proclamation must have been difficult for
Tutankhamun. No matter how he presented himself at court,
or how passionately he proclaimed his return to the old ways,
he knew that he was acting against the teachings of his father,
beliefs he'd grown up with and which were shared by his closest
family, most of whom were now dead. Aye, his closest adviser,
probably had similar feelings. He was one of the early adopters
of Akhenaten's new religious movement, proudly proclaiming
the king's teachings on the walls of his Amarna tomb. But
when the regime collapsed, like everyone else, he abandoned
the city.[22] Now, officially at least, Aye's allegiance lay firmly
with the traditional religion and to the young king. This had
served him well. He kept his job as head of the chariotry, and
his title of God's Father – reflecting his role as a close royal
adviser – and family connection to the royal line gave him
special influence at court. Wherever Tutankhamun went, Aye
followed – a reality captured by the king's artisans. In a scene
showing Tutankhamun ready to crack open the skull of an
enemy, watched by Ankhesenamun, Aye is there too.[23] It is also
possible that Aye eventually served Tutankhamun as vizier, the
highest office in the land.[24]

The job of executing the royal command to restore Egypt's temples fell to the treasury chief, Maya.[25] Maya had grown up at Akhenaten's court, served in his administration, and built a tomb for himself at Amarna. Like Aye (and, indeed, Tutankhamun himself), since the end of the Amarna interlude, Maya had dedicated himself to the traditional ways. As well as overseeing the treasury, he led all construction projects for the king, and organized the collection of taxes to fund the newly established temple projects.

Maya was assisted in his task by the chief sculptor and overseer of works Userhat-Hatiay,[26] who had lived at Amarna too (where everyone knew his house – his name was written on the door lintel). His work there had clearly impressed Akhenaten, because the king invited him to the palace and gave him the right to speak to him in private. Now, Userhat-Hatiay served Tutankhamun, who commanded him to replace or repair the images of the gods attacked under Akhenaten. Having spent his early life practising Akhenaten's new art style, carving the Aten, and hearing about the destruction of Amun's name, this was a dramatic change. It not only gave him the opportunity to travel to Egypt's neglected temples, but to craft anew the gods' sacred statues – their divine vessels on earth and the focal point of rituals. Kept in sanctuary shrines, these statues were quite small, but were made from precious materials, particularly gold, regarded as the skin of the gods. Priests treated these statues like lords in their mansions, making offerings to them three times each day, lavishing unguents and oils on them, and wrapping them in fine linen. Through the restoration or recreation of their statues, Tutankhamun was inviting the gods back into their homes, but it was Maya, and in particular Userhat-Hatiay, who provided the means to do so.

When Tutankhamun issued the command for restoration, the royal workshops buzzed with life. Stone was sculpted. Gems shaped. Gold hammered. Artisans travelled the country, re-carving the names of the gods wherever they'd been attacked and, where possible, repairing damaged statues. In one place, they found the faces on a statue of King Tuthmosis I, Queen Ahmose and Amun had been broken, as well as Amun's legs. The artists took another stone, carved replacement pieces from it, and fitted them into the statue, hiding the joins with plaster.[27]

11. The head of a statue of Tutankhamun.
A god's hand touches the back of his crown.

But due to the sheer amount of destruction that had taken place, they were forced to carve many statues from scratch. As was traditional, divine statues produced under a king bore an idealized royal portrait. Those made early in Tutankhamun's reign appear child-like, while later ones show him as a teenager. It was a strange turnaround: Tutankhamun had grown up under a father who hated Amun, sending out his followers to smash his statues wherever they stood. Now, Tutankhamun had to replace them, and Amun would bear his face.

The restoration also meant that vacant temple positions had to be filled. General Horemheb personally oversaw the appointment of Egypt's most influential priests,[28] despite his previous devotion to the Aten; earlier in life, he'd been Paatenemheb and owned a tomb at Amarna. He gave the role of high priest of Amun at Karnak – the most powerful priest after the king – to a man named Paranefer, who later changed his name to Wennefer. His original name, meaning 'the Perfect Name', had been a way of describing Akhenaten. The high priest must have been eager for the return to tradition, because he quickly commissioned a tomb at Thebes, though its artworks were heavily influenced by the Amarna style. Perhaps the artists he hired were trained under Akhenaten.[29] Other high priestly positions were quickly filled too. A man named Ptahemhat-Ty became high priest of Ptah at Memphis,[30] and Sainheret was installed as high priest of Re at Heliopolis.[31] Surprisingly, Tutankhamun allowed an Aten temple at Memphis to remain open. Its high priest, Meryneith, managed this temple early in the reign of Akhenaten, and then shared his time between the temple in Memphis and new duties as head of the Aten cult at Amarna. During that time, he changed his name to Meryre; but with his return to working solely in Memphis, and the Amarna Aten temples closed, he changed it back to Meryneith.[32]

THE REBURIAL OF TUTANKHAMUN'S AMARNA FAMILY

Having set in motion the restoration of the old religion, after three years as king Tutankhamun's thoughts turned to his family. The government had left Amarna and its inhabitants were abandoning the city. Even the dead were leaving. The artisans of the Workmen's Village exhumed their relatives from their Amarna graves and took them back to their traditional home at Deir el-Medina in Thebes.[33] The time had come for Tutankhamun's deceased relatives to leave too. The Valley of the Kings in Thebes had served as a royal burial ground since the time of King Tuthmosis I, 170 years before Tutankhamun, and had only lost its function under his father. With the return to tradition, reburial of his family in the sacred ground would be the perfect symbol of the king's renewed devotion to the old ways – and perhaps even help them to attain a true after-life with the gods. With his family members entombed in the Valley of the Kings it would regain the prime position as royal burial ground.

With his decision taken, the twelve-year-old Tutankhamun sent his servants to Amarna to collect his family members from the abandoned royal tomb east of the city. Their bodies were raised from their sarcophagi and their burial equipment dismantled, ready for the journey south to Thebes. Meanwhile, workmen dug a tomb for them in the Valley of the Kings, carving out a stairway and corridor, and a main chamber with a small storage room. Though they plastered the walls, they did not paint any scenes of the dead with the gods or inscribe any texts from afterlife books.[34] A plain tomb would have to do.

And because of the limited space, mortuary priests had to choose which items of burial equipment would join the bodies in the tomb. They decided to include four canopic jars of Queen Kiya, a gilded shrine of Queen Tiye, magic bricks for Akhenaten, a lion-headed funerary bed, and a wooden coffin made for Queen Kiya, but adapted for Akhenaten, whose body it now contained.[35] When the workmen had placed the burial goods and mummies inside, they sealed the tomb's entrance with blocks of stone and plastered over the doorway. The final step was for officials to stamp Tutankhamun's name in the wet plaster.[36] The king decided to bury his grandmother, Queen Tiye, in the tomb of her husband, King Amenhotep III, accompanied by shabti-figurines to magically perform work for her in the afterlife. In this tomb, she would be surrounded by the traditional decoration of a king.[37] Tutankhamun kept a

12. The coffin thought to have contained King Akhenaten's body.

lock of Tiye's hair in a set of nested coffins.[38] Although their lives had only briefly overlapped – she died while he was still very young – the relic served as a physical reminder of his grandmother.

TRAVEL AND FESTIVALS

Egypt's kings travelled frequently, often to attend religious festivals around the country. Although Tutankhamun was still young, he was no different. As the highest priest in the land, he visited temples and made offerings to the gods – keeping them happy was one of his major jobs, particularly given the events under his father. In this role, Tutankhamun dressed in the manner of a high priest, which, depending on the cult, could include a leopard skin worn over his shoulder. As a child, he wore a small fake leopard skin, made from linen, with an equally fake leopard head. When he was older, he exchanged this for a larger, true leopard skin, but again with a fake head.[39] Because Egypt's rituals and ceremonies could be complex, the young king was helped in his religious duties by his adviser Aye, who was awarded a special title that gave him the right to take part, despite not being a priest himself.[40]

On his journeys, the king stopped at royal rest houses, known as 'The mooring places of Pharaoh', and could bring along his own collapsible bedroom furniture. He had a fold-able wooden bed, and a similarly foldable headrest on which to place his head at night, made more comfortable by layers of linen.[41] During the day, when Tutankhamun sat outside, watching a festival or ritual, or just enjoying his time, his servants erected a collapsible canopy, on which they hung a sheet to protect him from the harsh sun. Beneath, he sat on a small stool, on a cushion filled with goose-feathers, carried to him by a servant using its leather straps.[42] When relaxing, he wore casual clothing, such as his tapestry-woven yellow tunic, decorated with blue and red stripes, hieroglyphs, and rows of walking and flying ducks.[43] During one trip to a temple, Tutankhamun needed help to walk – perhaps as a result of his clubfoot – and stepped down into the marshes to pull a sturdy reed from the ground to support himself. When the king touched an object, it became special, sharing in his divine power, so, once he no longer needed the reed, royal servants took it and embellished it with a gold covering, on which they wrote the story of how it came to be used by Tutankhamun. They then stored it among the king's possessions.[44]

One of the most important annual religious events that Tutankhamun attended was the Opet Festival at Thebes. Each year, from his coronation until his death, on the morning of the festival, Tutankhamun stepped out from his palace at Thebes and travelled to Karnak Temple, newly opened and refreshed, and once again inhabited by the king of the gods, Amun.[45] At the temple, his first stop was to stand before the three great model boats that would carry the statues of Amun, his wife Mut and son Khonsu 3 kilometres southwards to Luxor Temple. He made offerings to these gods, including food and wine, and recited the traditional prayers. The priests then raised the boats up, lifting them using long wooden poles, which they rested on their shoulders to spread the weight. Next, they walked in careful unison, led by Tutankhamun. The procession passed through the temple's grand gateway towards the Nile where, at the docks, the men loaded the gods' model boats onto real boats – one for each of the divine triad, one for the king and one for

Queen Ankhesenamun, whose boat accompanied that of the goddess Mut.[46]

The journey began. Men, walking along the banks of the Nile, pulled the boats by ropes, keeping them on course towards the temple of Luxor, and sang praises for the gods and Tutankhamun. The calm ripples of the Nile shimmered in the sunlight. Among the crowds, people fell to the floor and kissed the ground. Others raised their arms in adoration as the divinities passed them. Soldiers from Egypt, Nubia and Libya, carrying shields and armed with spears, bows and axes, marched along the riverbanks, following the gods and the royals in procession. The royal chariots, driven by attendants, accompanied them. Priests sang in honour of the king and Amun, while musicians played lyres, trumpets and clappers, followed by dancers. Men carried standards. Eventually, the boats reached the dock at Luxor Temple, where the gods received offerings of meat, birds, grapes and bread.

The king and the gods now entered Luxor Temple to perform the rituals of the Opet Festival. When the king stepped into the temple's Colonnade Hall, the noise of the crowds began to subside. Tutankhamun then continued into the Grand Sun Court, which formed the entrance to the most sacred inner parts of the temple.[47] Priests placed the boats of Mut and Khonsu within their own chambers, while others carried the boats of Amun and the king's royal ka-spirit deeper inside. Within the Chamber of the Divine King, priests poured water over Tutankhamun to purify him. Then, in the presence of Amun, watched by the god, they crowned the kneeling king, re-enacting the rituals performed at his coronation. Standing behind Tutankhamun, Amun touched the king's head, transferring the power of the royal ka into him. All that now remained was for Tutankhamun to make offerings to Amun in the barque sanctuary, where he was crowned once again.[48] The king, priests and gods then returned to their boats for the journey back to Karnak Temple, watched and celebrated by the people of Luxor. The rituals had renewed the king's divine power for another year.

To commemorate his role in this important annual event, Tutankhamun ordered his craftsmen to carve and paint scenes from the Opet Festival in the Colonnade Hall of Luxor Temple, featuring himself and Ankhesenamun.[49] As well as showing his piety to the gods, this act had an extra meaning. The construction of Luxor Temple had started under Amenhotep III, Tutankhamun's grandfather, so the work he commissioned there was a symbol of his devotion to his family, and a public pronouncement that he was a true successor, continuing the work that his family had begun. To emphasize this point, Tutankhamun gave credit for the work to Amenhotep III, rather than attempting to fully usurp the monument in his own name.

DIPLOMACY AND EMPIRE

Not all of Tutankhamun's duties were religious. It was also his responsibility to manage Egypt's empire, both to the south in Nubia, and to the north-east in the Levant – territories that had been held for decades – and to engage with the great kings beyond his own sphere of influence. Foreign delegations were not uncommon at the Egyptian court. People from across their known world brought expensive gifts to the palace, and as a traditional pharaoh, aiming to please the gods, Tutankhamun gave some of these treasures to the temples. Luxury goods brought from Punt were particularly prized, because their incense played an important role in temple rituals. When one trade delegation arrived from Punt, their exotic gifts were delivered straight to the Temple of Amun, where Tutankhamun personally presented them to the gods.[50] Other gifts, the king kept for himself, including a child-size Syrian tunic, decorated with an ankh-shaped collar and bands of complex geometric shapes at its edges. Some of these bands showed hunting, sphinxes and animals.[51] General Horemheb attended Egypt's diplomatic audiences, standing between the king and his foreign visitors, passing messages between the two with the help of an Egyptian translator.[52]

Diplomatic correspondence arrived in Egypt from kings across the Near East, whether vassals in the Levant or the powerful rulers of great kingdoms. On one occasion, a letter reached Tutankhamun's court from Burnaburiash, King of Babylon. He complained to Tutankhamun that the Egyptians had met with an Assyrian delegation, people that the Babylonians regarded as subjects.[53] This was a diplomatic faux-pas, and he wasn't pleased. But Tutankhamun knew – or at least had been instructed by his advisers – not to be too concerned. The great kings of the world often exaggerated their situations, both good and bad. It was true that the Egyptians had met with the Assyrians, opening diplomatic relations with them, but any threat posed by the Babylonians was remote and empty. If the Babylonians wanted to keep receiving gifts from the Egyptian court, they had to keep playing along.

Egypt's relationship with Nubia was different from that of other neighbouring regions. For hundreds of years, Nubia had been under direct Pharaonic control, and the Egyptians had expended great effort imposing their culture on this territory, incorporating it into their governmental system and building temples to their own gods. The region was rich in natural resources, particularly gold, and the Egyptians wanted to ensure their continued access. To keep Nubian rulers under control, the Egyptians took their children to the royal court, forcing them to grow up beside the Egyptian elite and learn Egyptian customs.[54] Tutankhamun himself may have spent his early years among some of the men who ruled parts of Nubia during his reign. Despite Egypt's grip, rebellions often broke out, inevitably leading to military reprisals. One Nubian uprising was defeated by General Horemheb, an event commemorated in a temple at Thebes by carvings of marching troops, an enemy run down by a chariot wheel, and bound prisoners.[55]

Years earlier, to manage the huge Nubian territory, the Egyptians created a new government post, the Viceroy of Kush. The holder of this office effectively behaved as another vizier, but with his remit entirely in the south.[56] Under Tutankhamun, the role of Viceroy of Kush was awarded to a man named Huy. Tutankhamun personally presided over his appointment, sitting enthroned for the occasion, though he did not speak. The task of leading the promotion ceremony fell to the overseer of the treasury, who handed Huy the Viceroy of Kush's official seal of office and announced to all present that he would control the land from Hierakonpolis in Egypt, southward to Napata in modern Sudan – a distance of around 735 kilometres. After receiving his promotion, Huy briefly travelled to the Temple of Amun at Karnak to make offerings before sailing south to Nubia to begin his work.[57]

Later, Huy returned to Tutankhamun's court bringing tribute from the south on heavily laden ships.[58] Tutankhamun led the reception ceremony, Blue Crown on his head, crook and flail in one hand, while servants laid out the wealth of Nubia before him. There were decorated shields, gold, a chariot, ebony, ivory tusks, stools, beds, thrones and bows. Huy had personally supervised the collection and loading of these items, supported by an array of assistants who collected, weighed and recorded the amounts gathered. Now, Huy stood in front of his offerings, cooling the king with an ostrich-feather fan. Nubian men knelt before the king, others walked, their arms heavy with gold. One group steered a giraffe into the royal presence. Others brought bulls. A Nubian princess rode a chariot pulled by cows.[59] Those present spanned Nubian society, from the princes and leaders of the Nubian regions down to prisoners of war – perhaps rebel leaders caught during Horemheb's campaign – still bound.

If Tutankhamun had been a little older, this event might have reminded him of his father's grand gathering at Amarna, when elaborate gifts, diplomats and prisoners from across the known world arrived at the royal court. For those who had been present at that event, it was perhaps the last time that Egypt felt prosperous – for a decade, life at court had been dominated by death and uncertainty. Now, things were improving. After a few years of rule, the young king was settling into his role. His education in the traditional ways was progressing, and he had gained valuable experience overseeing festivals, temple rituals and foreign affairs, guided by General Horemheb, his adviser Aye and the treasurer Maya. The teachings of Akhenaten were fading. Amarna was starting to sink beneath the sand.

Surely, at long last, nothing could stand in the way of Egypt's resurrection.

3

The Mortal God

The Great Pyramid of Khufu loomed high in the sky. Beside it was the Pyramid of Khafre, slightly smaller, but no less majestic, and a little further away, the Pyramid of Menkaure. Each had stood since around 2500 BC, over a thousand years before Tutankhamun's reign. These kings were remembered as great builders, and so, thought Tutankhamun, would he. He might not have built a huge pyramid, but he had dedicated his reign to restoring the favour of the gods, rebuilding their cults – something just as important. Their divine images, carved with his own idealized portrait, could now be found across Egypt and testified to his piety. While he rode on his chariot, elsewhere in the country, sculptors and artisans were busy re-carving the names of deities, repainting sacred words, putting precious stones back into place. The temples had reopened, priests were back at work, and his restorations would carry his name into eternity.

As he gazed up at the pyramids of Giza, he must have felt a connection with the already ancient kings who lay buried within. But he was not there to worship, he was there to enjoy himself. Earlier in his reign, Tutankhamun had commanded a small palace be built beside the Great Sphinx, a place where he could relax and launch his hunting expeditions, just like generations of his predecessors.[1] A stele erected between the Sphinx's paws proclaimed how it had chosen King Tuthmosis IV, his great-grandfather, for the kingship while he rested after a hunt at Giza – but only if he cleared the sand from around its leonine body. Tuthmosis had not been the next in line for the throne, but his act of piety brought the favour of the gods and launched him into power – at least, this is how he presented events.[2] Thanks to his own pious acts, Tutankhamun no doubt hoped for a long life in the gods' favour too.

After a youth spent working in their honour, and his earlier life of turbulence and loss, surely he deserved the chance to relax a little – to enjoy the time ahead of him.

MANAGING THE ROYAL HOUSEHOLD

Whether Tutankhamun was enjoying a carefree day of relaxation or preparing for government business, a whole administration existed to manage his life. General Horemheb held the title of high steward,[3] the palace administration's most senior role, but this was purely symbolic, and perhaps even a way for him to keep an eye on the king's activities. On a day-to-day basis, it was Ipy, the high steward in Memphis, who ran the palace and looked after Tutankhamun's private business, for it was there, in Memphis, that the king had his main residence. Ipy's father had passed the office of high steward to him towards the end of Amenhotep III's reign, and he later served Akhenaten in Amarna, where he owned a villa and built a tomb. After Tutankhamun came to power, he continued in office, but abandoned his Amarna property and built a new tomb at Saqqara.[4] When Ipy died, his office was awarded to Iniuia, a member of another elite family, who started his career as a scribe under the treasury chief Maya.[5] Though Ipy and then

Iniuia managed the overall palace business in Memphis, the king's private apartments had their own manager, Pay, whose father had grown up in the palace and had a close relationship with the royal family. Pay enjoyed court access throughout his life and, like Iniuia, was a friend of Maya.[6] In the end, it's all about who you know.

Below the elite staff at the top of the palace administration, Tutankhamun was attended by servants and scribes, among them his chief servant Tjay, the chief royal scribe Iny, and the scribe of his private apartments Panehesy. Other servants managed Tutankhamun's crowns and wardrobe. The royal laundry was supervised by Mahy,[7] and there was a special role for the man who managed the king's loincloths – of which Tutankhamun owned around 145.[8] The king's clothing ranged from plain to elaborate; there was something for every occasion. Early in his reign, the palace weavers had spent over a year carefully creating a tapestry-woven linen tunic for the young king. They wove a falcon at the neck, its outreached wings stretching over the shoulders, lotus flowers at the sides, and a blue lower section, embellished with rosettes of white, blue and red.[9] He also owned many pairs of sewn fibre sandals and open shoes of leather, decorated with beads. He wore these sandals so much that the weight of his body left marks on them, and the natural oils produced by his feet discoloured them.[10] Even in his late teens, Tutankhamun still owned his childhood clothes. Touched by the king, they had been infused with ritual power and could not be discarded.

Each day, to prepare him for his royal duties, Tutankhamun's servants washed him by pouring water over his body from behind a screen.[11] They took razors[12] and mirrors[13] from their designated boxes and carefully removed his stubble, before shaving the hair from his head. A bald head made it easier for him to wear a wig, over which they placed his diadem, fronted by a vulture and rearing cobra, its tail snaking across the top of his head to give it extra stability.[14] Earlier, Tutankhamun's servants had prepared his eye make-up by grinding galena or malachite and mixing it with water. They stored this make-up in tubes, into which they dipped a long stick, covering its tip so that they could apply it to his eyes.[15] They also rubbed sweet-smelling oils and unguents onto his skin. The king's unguents were stored in vessels of various materials and sizes, mostly carved from calcite.[16] One perfume jar was decorated with a lion lid – the lion sitting with his mouth open, showing his tongue.[17] One oil jar was carved in the shape of an ibex.[18]

Only after all this pampering was Tutankhamun ready to start his day's work – and there was much to be done.

13. A calcite cosmetic jar decorated with a lion.

A NEW YEAR CELEBRATION

It was mid-July, 1310 BC, and Egypt was busy celebrating the arrival of the new year.[19] Each year ended with a dangerous phase, when five days were added to the 360-day calendar. Though these five days were the birthdays of gods and goddesses, they existed beyond the traditional calendar, bringing the potential for disorder. Dangerous forces could sweep the land, causing sickness and death. To stay safe, people performed rituals on each day leading into the new year, and in particular, hoped to gain the favour of the goddess Sekhmet, who had the power to both spread and protect from disease. On the evening of the final day of the year, before the five birthdays of the gods, families enjoyed meals with their deceased relatives in the cemeteries.[20] They burned incense before statues of the dead, and wrapped them in new linen.[21] On the following five days, they collected water from the Nile, representing the renewal of life,[22] and lit candles.[23] When the new year safely arrived, the Egyptians regarded it as a cosmic renewal. The old year was over, and the sun god was reborn.[24] As a result, the first day of the new year was marked by the birthday of Re-Horakhety.[25] With so much going on, the whole new year festival lasted nine days; there was the final day of the old year, the five extra days, and the first three of the new year, which were treated as holidays.[26]

For Tutankhamun, an important duty on the first day of the new year was his reception of gifts.[27] These were brought to the palace by Egypt's highest courtiers, who acted as representatives of the royal workshops that produced them,[28] and foreign dignitaries. While the king sat enthroned, nobles from home and abroad paid their respects.[29] Servants carried each gift in procession, placing them on the floor before the royal throne dais, and scribes noted down everything received for the palace records.[30] Among the gifts were staffs, made of ebony, embellished with gold and silver or electrum,[31] chariots and bows, gold collars, chests, vases, tables, chairs, vessels made of glass, calcite and metal, bows and arrows, shrines, mirrors, shields, scale armour, daggers, statuettes of the king and queen, ritual beds and fans.[32] The scribes' hands must have grown tired from making their lists. Following tradition, Tutankhamun also gave gifts to his courtiers, selected from among those displayed before him. Often, these included linen and statues.[33] As was usual after a grand festival or event, a royal banquet was held once the rituals and ceremonies had ended.

When the evening came, servants lit lamps in the palace's banqueting hall. Their gentle flickering sent shadows dancing. The teenage king sat alongside Ankhesenamun, and the courtiers took their positions at their own small tables. Couples sat together, while singles were separated according to their sex. As this wasn't a ritual event, Tutankhamun decided to wear a white linen tunic decorated with red and blue stripes,[34] his waist wrapped with a woven tapestry sash bearing geometric shapes and hieroglyphs.[35] Over his chest, hanging on straps of gold and lapis lazuli, with beads of gold and glass, was a pectoral of the vulture goddess Nekhbet formed of lapis lazuli, carnelian, glass and gold.[36] On his arms, his bracelets shone with images of scarabs and cobras,[37] while his rings were decorated with the Eye of Horus and rosettes. Dangling from his ears, his earrings featured tassels of precious stones.[38] Because of his clubfoot, to make the evening more comfortable, he wore shoes with straps over his toes and extra material at their sides.[39] For Tutankhamun, this was a night of casual dress.

Behind the scenes, an army of staff had spent hours preparing meals. They made fried or baked bread in all manner of shapes.

They slaughtered animals and fried the meat in oil. They made dishes of duck breasts and wings, ox meat, geese, chickpeas, fenugreek, lentils, spices, honey and almonds.[40] Because banqueters ate with their hands, servants rushed around the hall, pouring water over their fingers to clean them. Tutankhamun himself poured water over Ankhesenamun's hands.[41] Meanwhile, the king's servants brought him food from the temple, ritually purified, and suitable for a god. Occasionally, he ordered a servant to give one of these special dishes to a favoured courtier. To receive food from the king's table was an honour, something that might even be mentioned in a person's tomb inscriptions.[42]

Beer and wine flowed without end, and Tutankhamun himself sat and sipped from fine chalices.[43] The king owned vineyards across Egypt, looked after by dedicated staff who ensured the grapes were picked, trodden, and pressed. When servants carried the wine amphorae into the banqueting hall,

14. Tutankhamun pouring water on the hand of Ankhesenamun.

the king and his staff inspected the name of the chief vintner written on the pottery, along with the type of wine, the year it was produced and where. Some amphorae were produced by the chief vintner Khaa, others by Sennufe and Rer:[44] three types were available: red, white, and a filtered and heated red wine called shedeh, which was popular among the guests.[45] Each time servants opened a new amphora, they broke off the clay plug in the spout. For those guests without a taste for wine, beer was served, or fruit juice. While waiting to be opened, the amphorae were stacked in a corner of the hall, beside a troupe of musicians.[46] The walls were decorated with grape vines and flowers, and the air was filled with the sound of flutes and harps. Trumpets sounded. Women sat on the ground playing instruments, while singers sang songs, sometimes about the king, clapping the rhythm with their hands. Other women danced, clapping their hands and performing acrobatics before the guests.

15. A lotus chalice decorated with Tutankhamun's royal names.

When the banquet ended, Tutankhamun relaxed by playing games and listening to stories told to the court. Among his entertainment options was senet, a popular game with a board of thirty squares, and another game that had twenty squares. In both cases, he threw knucklebones or casting sticks to determine his moves. One set of Tutankhamun's casting sticks was made from ebony and ivory, another was of ivory, carved with Asiatic and Nubian prisoners. Two of the king's game boards were designed for travel, and had drawers built into them for storing his game pieces. One of these bore an image of himself, enthroned with

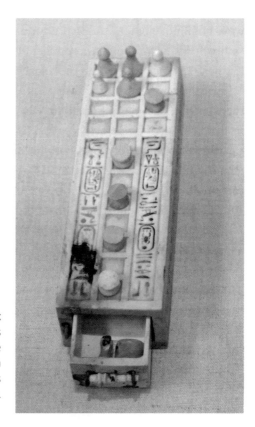

16. A game box with drawers to store the pieces, from Tutankhamun's tomb.

Ankhesenamun standing before him, lotus flower in hand.[47] Perhaps the two played this game together when travelling around Egypt.[48]

After a full day of rituals, celebrations and entertainment, Tutankhamun went to bed. His private chambers were at the rear of the palace, behind his busy audience hall and the administrative offices beyond. Only in sleep was he hidden from the world, alone, except for Ankhesenamun beside him and the bodyguard stationed outside his bedroom. As Tutankhamun shifted in bed, his legs and feet scratched tiny fragments of gilding from the wood.[49] If he wished, when the morning came, he could describe his dreams to a professional interpreter, who would tell him whether they were good or bad omens for his future.[50] For now though, there was nothing to worry about. His headrest, decorated with the household god Bes,[51] fought off nightmares. Scenes of nature painted on the palace walls recreated the moment of creation, when all the cosmos was in balance. There were symbols of life and protection, and carvings of defeated enemies kept the forces of chaos away. Magically, his home was infused with order, under the protection of the gods.[52]

Tutankhamun slept a peaceful night.

THE BURIAL OF AN APIS BULL

The Apis bull had spent its life pampered in Memphis, kept in its own enclosure and worshipped as an incarnation of the creator god Ptah. Few bulls in history have had it so good. Now, as Tutankhamun entered his late teens,[53] it was dead and another bull had to be selected to replace it. To identify the next incarnation, the Memphite priests had specific requirements: each bull needed to have the same markings, namely to be black, but with a white diamond on top of its head. On its tongue, there had to be a beetle pattern, while on its back, the shape of an eagle.[54] This was an old tradition – the connection between Ptah and the Apis bull had existed for around 1,700 years by Tutankhamun's reign.[55] Now, it was the teenage king's turn to perform the solemn burial rituals, just as his father and grandfather had done before him. It was an extra royal duty, on top of the many audiences and festivals that he already had to lead.

First though, a suitable monument had to be created in the bull's honour. Tutankhamun's craftsmen dug out a large chamber beneath the ground of the ancient necropolis at Saqqara, leaving it undecorated. A corridor connected this room with the surface, exiting in a chapel on a platform, itself reached by a flight of steps.[56] Meanwhile, embalmers set to work mummifying the bull. They removed its internal organs, just as they did with humans, and placed them in four huge canopic jars.[57] The bull was then lowered into a wooden coffin, ready for burial.[58] When the time came to perform the funerary rituals at Saqqara, Tutankhamun wore a 'stole' or religious scarf of faience beads, which bore inscriptions naming the Memphite gods Sokar and Ptah,[59] and he left royal gifts of faience pendants for the bull.[60] Once the king completed the rituals, the tomb was sealed, and the search for the new Apis bull began.

That evening, as Tutankhamun travelled back to his palace in Memphis, carried in his palanquin, his thoughts turned to events in a land far from home. Weeks earlier, his troops had left for Syria, aiming to recapture territory lost to Egypt a decade before. Had his daily rituals, and now his offerings to the Apis bull, pleased the gods enough to ensure their favour in this critical campaign?

WAR AGAINST THE HITTITES

When General Horemheb stood on the plains of Syria, looking towards the city of Qadesh, he must have felt a combination of duty and dread.[61] The city had fallen under Egyptian control during the reign of King Tuthmosis III, a pharaoh who had campaigned widely and was more responsible than any pharaoh for Egypt's influence in the Near East. It had remained part of their empire for centuries – that is, until the time of Akhenaten. During his reign, the Hittites, a people from eastern Turkey, had entered a new expansionist phase, moving beyond their normal territory. The Egyptian vassal at Qadesh, a minor king named Shutatarra, had provoked their army. The Hittites attacked and the city fell. With this miscalculation, Qadesh, a major centre on the trade routes of the northern Levant, was lost to Egypt and the empire shrank accordingly. The Hittites swiftly replaced Shutatarra with his son, Aitakama, who publicly proclaimed allegiance to Egypt, whilst supporting the Hittites. Akhenaten had eventually acted, and sent a force to Qadesh to deal with the problem, but it was unsuccessful.[62]

Tutankhamun inherited these problems. He knew that the loss of Qadesh was an embarrassment for the Egyptians, and it was up to him to set the record straight. But despite his hunting experience, array of weaponry, and leather armour,[63] he was still a teenager, and not yet skilled enough to lead an army. In his place, he sent out Horemheb. A career military man, Horemheb knew the feel of battle, and the value of Qadesh, whose fortified walls now rose up above him on a mound. The terrain around him was very different from that of Egypt. The Mediterranean sea was 50 kilometres to the west, the direction of death in Egyptian belief, rather than the usual north; there were many rivers, including the Orontes which curved its path around Qadesh and connected with a stream, giving the city the impression of standing on an island. The terrain was much hillier than Egypt and there were trees all around, with woods to march troops through – something not present back home.[64] Horemheb's army, as it camped in the vicinity of Qadesh, was split into divisions, with charioteers, archers and infantry, all fighting in the name of Egypt's gods. At the centre of the camp stood the command tent, where Horemheb planned his attack strategy.[65] All were prepared for battle, and to correct past mistakes.

Whatever happened that day at Qadesh, and indeed, at earlier battles in the campaign, cannot be reconstructed in any detail. But when the Egyptians returned home by sea, waves splashed Aitakama in the face as he dangled from a cage on the royal boat. He was now a prisoner of the pharaoh.[66] Along the way, the Egyptian troops, tired and resting, thought back to what they'd witnessed: charioteers riding valiantly into battle; Hittites falling to their deaths from a fortress, while Egyptians climbed ladders up its walls, spears in hand and shields over their shoulders; Egyptians marching with severed enemy hands impaled on their spears. Later, such memories were captured in stone – both Tutankhamun and Horemheb capitalized on the campaign by commissioning artists to carve grand war scenes in its commemoration.[67] But despite all the celebration and bombast, one thing is clear: Qadesh ultimately remained in Hittite hands. If the Egyptians captured the city, it quickly reverted back to enemy control. And the Egyptian assault was swiftly succeeded by a Hittite campaign into Egyptian territory. Tutankhamun's campaign, then, met with limited success.

Once home in Egypt, Horemheb paraded his prisoners of war in the palace before the enthroned Tutankhamun and

Ankhesenamun. The royal couple looked down from their dais at the Levantine men, women and children assembling before them.[68] The men's hands were bound as they were dragged along. Small children were raised up on their parents' shoulders, or carried in slings on their backs. At the front of this cruel parade, Horemheb received rewards from the king for his excellent service to the crown.[69] As Horemheb stood, arms upraised, servants placed collars of gold around his neck, while others waited to bring him more. If the campaign to Qadesh had indeed been a failure, it appears to have somehow worked out well for Horemheb,[70] who enjoyed even more prestige than before.

After rewarding Horemheb, it was important for Tutankhamun to thank the gods for the campaign's success – even if it was limited. The Egyptian army had brought the spoils of war back to the court, and it was traditional for a share to be given to the deities in their temples. At Karnak, Tutankhamun entered the Temple of Amun, where newly carved statues of the god, his wife, Mut, and son, Khonsu, awaited. Opening the shrines, their faces, now made in the likeness of the young king, stared back at him. Along with the items seized in the Levant, servants dragged prisoners of war into the gods' presence – perhaps some were the same people earlier brought before Tutankhamun by Horemheb. The majority of these prisoners would be sent to work on Amun's estates, but it's possible that the king ceremonially executed a few of them before the gods, transforming them into symbols of Egypt's defeat of chaos and the restoration of order. This act was a strong sign of the pharaoh's devotion to Amun – a symbol that the dark days of Akhenaten had finally been expunged from memory.

THE HUNT

Having executed his enemies, the king had again earned a chance to relax. It was time to kill some animals instead. In the marshes beside the Nile, Tutankhamun sat on a low stool, his arms raised holding his bow. His arrow pointed ahead, his target in sight. Ankhesenamun sat below the king on a cushion, holding out his next arrow. All around, birds lay dead, pierced through their chests. Others hid among the papyrus plants, nervously waiting for the coast to be clear. Beside Tutankhamun, his pet lion sauntered along, hoping to grab a dead bird for himself.[71] Tutankhamun owned a variety of bows, including one decorated with the heads of his enemies at its tips; each time he pulled the bowstring, he strangled them.[72] He stored some of these in an elaborate bow-case, decorated with hunting scenes.[73] Later in the day, the royal couple boarded a papyrus boat, and sailed through the marshes, continuing their hunt. This time, they decided to use a curved throw stick, which Tutankhamun prepared to hurl, while gripping the birds they'd already sent to Osiris in his other hand.[74] It was a normal day out for the king and queen – a happy distraction from the increasing requirements of government now that they were older.

On another occasion, Tutankhamun hunted ostriches near Heliopolis. Craftsmen took the feathers from his kills and attached them to a fan, which his servants wafted to keep him cool during the heat of the day.[75] In this, the king was following in the footsteps of one of his royal ancestors, Tuthmosis III, who caught seventy-five ostriches during a single hunt.[76] Lions, leopards and hyenas were among the most dangerous animals hunted by Egypt's kings, while for an easier day out, there were the less life-threatening gazelles and antelopes.[77] For close combat, whether against dangerous animals or enemies,

Tutankhamun owned clubs and maces,[78] and a selection of curving khepesh-swords, including a small, light one that he wielded when young.[79] He also had slings, which he used to launch pebbles at high speed at doomed creatures.[80] For protection, he wore leather scale armour and held shields.[81] But he was rarely unsafe. Servants often forced the most dangerous animals into pens, making it easier for the pharaohs to rain arrows upon them from a distance – and then boast about the high numbers they'd personally killed.[82]

Perhaps the greatest thrill came from hunting on a chariot, speeding along after fleeing animals, one man steering the horses, the other firing arrows. Tutankhamun rode two of his hunting chariots so frequently that his staff had to replace parts of their wheels; one of them was built to cope with difficult terrain, and so was particularly suited to hunting expeditions.[83] Tutankhamun's love of hunting by chariot led him to order his artisans to paint the lid of one of his wooden chests with colourful scenes of him chasing down animals.[84] On one side of the lid, the king, standing alone on his chariot, races across a desert plain, his bow raised, an arrow ready to fire. His two horses rear, wearing headdresses and elaborate back coverings, their hooves about to trample the fleeing animals ahead. To the side of the horses, one of Tutankhamun's hunting dogs bites into the rear of an unfortunate antelope. Two other dogs have run ahead and clamped their mouths around the necks of other antelopes. Ostriches, a hyena, donkeys and antelopes flee in terror. On the other side of the lid, the artists painted a second scene in which Tutankhamun chases down fallen lions, each pierced with arrows from his bow.[85] His artisans were also ordered to carve similar desert hunting scenes – describing or showing him chasing bulls, antelope and lions – on the walls of one of his temples.[86]

17. One of the six chariots found in Tutankhamun's tomb. The king probably rode it on ceremonial occasions.

18. Tutankhamun hunting while riding on his chariot, painted on the lid of one of the chests found in his tomb.

Hunting, then, was of great importance to Tutankhamun. It was a way for him to relax with Ankhesenamun, to prove his ability as a warrior, and an activity that he wanted immortalized in art. His hunting and killing of wild animals also had a divine dimension: it represented the king's power to impose order over chaos.

It would also be one of the last things that he would ever do.

TUTANKHAMUN'S DEATH

It was while out hunting one day in August 1310 BC that Tutankhamun fell from his chariot.[87] He crashed into the ground. He felt his left leg snap. Blood poured from the split. Pain surged through his body. When his servants rushed over and saw his broken leg, they immediately carried him inside the palace and summoned the best doctors in Egypt. As he lay on his bed, Ankhesenamun close by his side, the doctors gave him opium and water lilies to ease his pain,[88] and priests of Sekhmet warded off dangerous demons that could infect his body.[89] Given his problems walking and his recurring bouts of malaria,[90] which often left him feeling sick and weak, Tutankhamun had frequently needed to consult the palace doctors. There was usually nothing to fear. But on this day, the look in their eyes made him nervous.

Following their training and the writings in the medical papyri,[91] before the royal doctors could help the king, they first had to place his injury into one of three categories, deciding whether it was a problem that they could certainly treat, one that might be treatable, or one that was a lost cause. The senior doctor leaned down to take a look at the king's broken leg. Using his hands to examine the open wound, he felt and heard the sound of the fractured bone. The king screamed in pain. The extent of the break and the amount of blood pouring from it made any chance of healing Tutankhamun unlikely. It was a bleak diagnosis.

The royal doctors knew that nothing could be done. Normally, in such circumstances, the patient couldn't be helped. But this was no ordinary patient. None of them wanted to be responsible for the young king's death, so they acted quickly. First, they soaked linen in oil and honey and placed it on the wound. The honey helped to dry out the injury, and had the added benefit that it scared away the demons that caused illness.[92] Then they wrapped the leg with linen and alum, which had an antiseptic quality.[93] The wrappings stopped the king's leg from moving, holding it in place like a splint. Beyond this, there was nothing they could do, but wait.[94]

As time passed, the doctors' worst fears were realized. The king's fractured leg became infected. Tutankhamun weakened. His body was unable to fight the infection. The nineteen-year-old pharaoh was dying.[95]

Tutankhamun faded away.

4

Preparing for a Journey

Tutankhamun awoke in death. Although he had died at only nineteen, an eternity remained before him. When he arrived in the afterlife, he cast his mind back to what had happened to him in his final days. The fall from his chariot. The crunch and limpness in his leg. The rush to get him to the palace doctors. The infection that wouldn't heal. The panic in people's eyes. And then, the darkness. Now the pain was over, and his second life could begin. He would not rest in peace.

Tutankhamun's afterlife would be a time of combat, with the fate of the cosmos relying on his success. Each sunset, he would join the sun god – now weak and old, having aged over the course of the day – on his night boat and sail beneath the horizon through the Duat, the afterlife realm. He and the sun god, merged as one identity, would descend through this dangerous domain of rivers, fields, and deserts, on a quest for resurrection. As they travelled, they would be assisted by gods and demons, and offer help to the spirits of the blessed dead. But there was danger too. Apophis, the chaos snake, along with his followers, sought to plunge the world into disorder. Only by reaching the sixth hour of the night, when the sun god merged with Osiris' regenerative force, could these enemies be defeated and a new day begin at dawn. If Tutankhamun had felt stressed in his short life as king, it was nothing compared to his destiny in the afterlife.

Yet even this busy afterlife was not assured. Tutankhamun could only succeed in his eternal mission if those left living completed his funerary rituals properly and supplied him with an extensive burial assemblage. The mummification of his body, the ritual items placed in his tomb, and even the tomb decoration itself, would all serve to give him eternal life. If any part of the rituals were skipped, or if his funerary goods were lacking, he would experience the second death. True death. His fate rested in the hands of the living – and they were having their own problems.

THE FUTURE

From the moment of her husband's death in August, the twenty-year-old Ankhesenamun became the last survivor of her royal line. As senior royal, she held power while decisions were taken on who would succeed Tutankhamun.[1] The kingship desperately needed stability. The cosmos and Egypt's success relied on there being a pharaoh to act as intermediary between the people and the gods. Would Ankhesenamun take the throne as king herself? Nefertiti had ruled as Neferneferuaten, and earlier, Hatshepsut had elevated herself from queen to king. On this occasion though, the court preferred that Ankhesenamun marry. Perhaps they envisioned that a child would ensue, extending the dynasty just a little longer.

Ankhesenamun made it clear that she wouldn't marry someone from her own entourage. She wanted to find a royal personage, and in Egypt, there weren't any left. Her solution was unconventional: she wrote a letter to the Hittite King Suppululiuma I. Aiming to reach Egypt's enemy as fast as possible, the queen's messenger left Memphis, crossed the Sinai and headed north through Egypt's Levantine territory. His destination was Hattusa, the Hittite capital in Turkey, but along the way, he heard that the Hittite king was besieging the city of Carchemish in Syria and adapted his route. Within two weeks of leaving Egypt, he stood at the Hittite camp, letter in hand. It was now September.

When Suppiluliuma I heard what was written in the queen's letter, he probably demanded that it be read out again. She was asking him if he had a son that she could marry: a man who would become pharaoh. To this, the Hittite court was understandably sceptical. Both Ankhesenamun's father and husband had launched military campaigns against them. Relations had been frosty for over a decade, though a treaty had since been established between the two powers. Perhaps, then, things could improve further? If Egypt and the Hittites united, the resulting empire would stretch from Sudan, through Egypt, around the Levant, and northwards into eastern Turkey. It would be a formidable power – a world empire before world empires existed.

It was surely a tempting offer, but given the oddness of the situation, before making a decision, Suppiluliuma decided to send his envoy, Hattusaziti, to Egypt to investigate and learn more about what had happened. This was not what Ankhesenamun wanted to hear. By the time the Hittite fact-finding mission arrived in Egypt, two more weeks had passed, and even more time would be needed to convince Hattusaziti of her sincerity. It was already late September, making it impossible for him to return to Hattusa and report to Suppiluliuma before the winter snows blocked passage to the city in late October. Because of the Hittite mistrust, there would be no royal burial and no royal successor until after the winter. While these events played out, and Egypt's future remained uncertain, preparations for Tutankhamun's burial continued.

GATHERING AND CRAFTING THE TOMB'S TREASURES

To ensure a king's survival in the afterlife, Egypt's priests stocked the royal tombs in the Valley of the Kings with a variety of standardized ritual items.[2] The royal artisans normally began producing these early in the king's reign, but with the restoration of the divine cults and temples diverting their attention, little was ready by the time of Tutankhamun's death. Unaware of the delays that would be caused by the Hittite envoy's investigation, the artisans expected to have just seventy days to craft the necessary equipment – seventy days being the traditional time from a pharaoh's death to his burial. This didn't give them much time. Luckily, there was a ready source of royal grave goods to draw from: the unused treasures prepared for Neferneferuaten, which had sat in storage since her death.

Rifling through Neferneferuaten's burial assemblage, the artisans chose items that they could recycle in Tutankhamun's name. Among them, they took small coffins made to contain her mummified internal organs and a pectoral of the goddess Nut,[3] but one item in particular caught their attention: her spectacular gold death mask. Taking it back to their workshop, they adapted her cartouches so that they spelled out Tutankhamun's names and replaced her face with the boy king's own official image.[4] This work, and that on the tomb's many other gold objects, was supervised by Ameneminet, who managed Tutankhamun's goldsmiths.[5] The artisans also took Neferneferuaten's red quartzite sarcophagus,[6] which had been decorated over a decade earlier. To update the decoration, each sculptor took a side of the sarcophagus basin, and set to work re-carving the details. Over the course of two months, they changed the names and added long wings to the goddesses standing at its corners. All traces of previous ownership had to be removed before Tutankhamun could be placed within.[7] Meanwhile, other artisans shaped a block of granite to serve as the sarcophagus' lid. On its gently sloping surface, they carved inscriptions for the gods Anubis, Thoth and the winged sun disc Behdety.[8]

To add to the tomb content, the artisans collected objects used by Tutankhamun in life or that were kept in the palace storerooms. They grabbed storage vessels, a soapstone scarab and a persea fruit made from glass, all from the time of King Tuthmosis III,[9] a century before Tutankhamun. Other items had a more personal significance. They earmarked for burial the nested coffins containing Queen Tiye's lock of hair that Tutankhamun had cherished in life;[10] a pair of clappers, inscribed

19. Tutankhamun's sarcophagus in his burial chamber. Carved goddesses stretch out their wings in protection.

with the names of Queen Tiye and Tutankhamun's half-sister, Princess Meritaten; and one of Meritaten's scribal palettes, which bore an inscription mentioning Queen Nefertiti.[11] Other objects probably belonged to Akhenaten, including a skullcap that would eventually be placed on Tutankhamun's head.[12] Tutankhamun's two stillborn children were also selected to be placed in the tomb. These had been mummified and placed in two tiny coffins, kept together in a plain wooden box,[13] though the craftsmen had to cut down the feet on one of the coffins to make it fit inside.[14]

Courtiers donated items too. Maya, the overseer of the treasury, gave a shabti – a magical statuette that would come alive and perform tasks in place of Tutankhamun in the afterlife – and a small bier surmounted by a mummy.[15] A general named Nakhtmin – perhaps Aye's son – gave five shabtis.[16] A vizier gave a jar of wine.[17] As servants packed Tutankhamun's possessions into boxes – whether gold grasshoppers, a silver milk jug, gold rings, or clothes and mosquito nets given by the servants who looked after the king's bedroom – scribes carefully labelled them, ready for transportation.[18]

Among the objects specially crafted for Tutankhamun's burial were thirty-four statuettes of the king and gods, each made from wood and placed on a pedestal. They included Atum of Heliopolis, Ptah of Memphis, and the goddesses Isis and Nephthys. Two statuettes of Tutankhamun showed him standing on a papyrus boat, holding his spear in the air, perhaps ready to kill a hippopotamus – a symbol of the god Seth. Two other statuettes showed him standing on a leopard,[19] though the craftsmen only had to carve one, as its doppelgänger was taken from among Neferneferuaten's treasures.[20] Working fast to reach their tight deadline, the artisans wrote the names of the king and gods on the statuettes' bases with little thought for finesse or care[21] – as long as the names were legible, it was good enough. The craftsmen then prepared shrines to house the statuettes. In the meantime they were stored away, ready for the funeral, wrapped in linen left over from the time of Akhenaten, with tiny flower garlands placed on their heads.[22] At this point, they found that the statuette of the goddess Sekhmet wouldn't fit into the shrine made for her, so an artisan had to saw off the front of the base, accidentally losing the goddess' sceptre in the process.[23]

20. Two statuettes of Tutankhamun standing on a leopard, as they appeared when discovered by Howard Carter.

PREPARING THE TOMB CHAMBERS

The men responsible for getting Tutankhamun's tomb ready in time for his burial were well known to him in life: the overseer of the treasury, Maya,[24] and the craftsman Userhat-Hatiay who had spearheaded the restoration effort.[25] Their first job was to visit the Valley of the Kings and decide where to bury the young pharaoh, given that his own tomb, under construction in the western valley, was nowhere near complete.[26] After exploring the valley's dry riverbeds, and with little time to spare, they chose to adapt a tomb made for the royal adviser, Aye. As a respected noble with connections to the royal family, Aye had been granted the favour of a burial in the Valley of the Kings and work had been ongoing for years. By the time of Tutankhamun's death, Aye had an undecorated, two-chamber tomb waiting for him.[27] This wouldn't do for a king: it needed to be a little grander before Tutankhamun could be buried within.

Upon receiving their orders, the royal craftsmen mobilized to transform Aye's tomb. They worked eight consecutive days in the valley, spending each night sleeping in a small settlement on site, before descending the hills for two days of rest with their families at Deir el-Medina – the state-managed settlement where they lived. This weekly walk – a long uphill march and then the reverse – left them with painful cases of osteoarthritis in their ankles and knees,[28] which must have led to much grumbling, particularly when carrying heavy equipment. In the tomb, the craftsmen had to chisel out what would become Tutankhamun's burial chamber, excavating it at a lower level than the existing rooms, and carving out beside it an extra chamber – the one that would be later known as the treasury.[29] There was no space to craft the long descending corridor that typically gave access to a royal tomb, or to significantly expand the tomb's design.

Slowly, the workmen hacked out the shape of the burial chamber using flint or chert tools. Two teams, each with their own side of the chamber and their own supervisors, worked simultaneously. Limestone dust covered their faces and hands and floated like mist in the air as they chipped away at the walls. Servants carried stone rubble and flakes outside in baskets and dumped them away from the tomb entrance. Once the craftsmen had cut out the rough shape of the room, they smoothed the walls and floor with copper and bronze tools, but not the ceiling. They then used trowels and their hands to plaster the walls, leaving imprints of their fingers, in preparation for the paintings.[30] It was tiring work, particularly in a stuffy tomb in the heat of the day, but the artisans were happy to have returned to Deir el-Medina after having been forced, under Akhenaten, to abandon it for Amarna. These talented artists had not only left behind the houses where their ancestors had lived for generations, but had also lost their greatest canvas, the Valley of the Kings. Thankfully, it was only temporary.

MUMMIFICATION AND RITUALS

While artisans adapted Aye's tomb for Tutankhamun, the young king's body lay on an embalming table, probably at Thebes. Earlier, servants and priests had escorted his corpse across the Nile in a coffin, a symbolic journey that reflected his movement from the east side of the river, representing life, to the west side, associated with death. When Tutankhamun's body arrived on the western shore, priests made offerings to him, while priestesses, representing the goddesses Isis and Nephthys, mourned and killed a bull that represented Seth, murderer of

Osiris.[31] From the riverbank, they continued their procession to the embalming place, which was near Tutankhamun's mortuary temple.

The embalmers gathered around Tutankhamun's body. They were about to start a process that would take seventy days – the same length of time that the star Sirius vanished from the night sky each year. Its reappearance marked the beginning of the new year, a rebirth, just as Tutankhamun would experience in the afterlife. To ensure this rebirth though, they had to remove his body from time and its decay. They would transform him into an eternal ritual image, a vessel in which his soul could rest and recharge. Should his body be lost or destroyed, the dead king would have to rely on statues bearing his name for his survival, which would not be as ritually powerful.

Tutankhamun's body was washed and purified for three days, before being moved to the embalming chamber.[32] There, the embalmers removed his brain through his nose and discarded it, and poured resin twice into his skull – once while the king lay on his back, and another time while he was upside down.[33] To reach and remove his internal organs, they made a cut across his belly. They left the king's diaphragm intact, although it was normal to break this when removing the lungs.[34] They also removed his heart,[35] even though this was usually left in the body. The heart was essential for a person to achieve an afterlife, because it was weighed against the feather of Maat in the judgement hall of Osiris to determine their fate. Once extracted, Tutankhamun's internal organs were individually mummified and placed in small coffins, each with its own compartment in his canopic chest. The embalmers poured a mixture of resin and unguents into these compartments, filling the space around the coffins.[36] They next inserted linen, soaked in resin, into Tutankhamun's body cavities, and shaved his body

21. The lids of the four compartments in Tutankhamun's canopic chest. His internal organs were kept in small coffins within each compartment.

and head.[37] After placing the king's arms on his stomach,[38] they covered his body with a type of salt called natron, which would dry out the corpse, preventing it from decaying.

After forty days, the embalmers removed the natron and washed Tutankhamun's body. It was time to begin the wrapping process. They took long strips of linen and began by carefully bandaging his fingers, toes, legs, arms, torso and head. This ensured that his body remained whole, for a damaged or incomplete body would be similarly damaged or incomplete in the afterlife. They mummified his penis erect, perhaps to associate him with the god of regeneration, Osiris.[39] The embalmers then poured jars of unguent over Tutankhamun, while uttering spells and wrapping him. Between the layers of linen strips, they added amulets of magical power, pectorals, necklaces and other jewellery. Unusually, they didn't include a heart scarab in the king's wrappings, even though it was normal to place one over the chest.[40] Next, they slid gold coverings over each finger and toe,[41] rings over the finger stalls, and bracelets on his arms.[42]

When completing their work, the embalmers put two daggers on Tutankhamun's body. One at his waist, and the other at his right thigh. This second dagger was particularly special, for its blade was formed of meteoritic iron and it was perhaps a gift from the king of the Mitanni to Amenhotep III, Tutankhamun's grandfather.[43] They also placed Akhenaten's skullcap, decorated with rearing cobras, on top of the king's head, and above it, a gold vulture and uraeus. They hid these beneath layers of wrappings and the royal diadem, which itself was covered with linen and padding.[44] After the addition of gold hands on the mummy bundle, gripping the crook and flail as symbols of royal power, they lowered the final ritual item into place: the gold mask, which would keep Tutankhamun eternally young.

Once Tutankhamun was mummified, there were further rituals to perform. These included a nightly vigil in which priests and priestesses, playing the parts of different deities, protected Tutankhamun, who represented Osiris, from attacks by the god Seth. Other rituals symbolically took the mummy

22. A dagger from Tutankhamun's tomb.

on journeys to sacred locations around Egypt.[45] Meanwhile, the embalmers gathered up whatever mummification material had been used – linen, spare natron, leftover floral collars, sawdust, the fabric worn on the embalmers' heads – and placed them in large pots.[46] As ritually charged items, these would later join the funerary procession.

23. Tutankhamun's gold mask, found on the king's mummy.

THE PRINCE OF HATTUSA

The winter snows that blocked access to Hattusa had melted in the mountains. The Hittite king, Suppiluliuma, waited impatiently for the return of his envoy, Hattusaziti.[47] Did the Egyptians really expect him to send a son? Would a Hittite become pharaoh? When the messenger finally arrived, he came with an Egyptian envoy named Hani and a letter from Ankhesenamun. The queen's letter expressed her outrage that the king had not trusted her words. She reiterated: her husband was dead. She did not have a son. Send a prince and he will become pharaoh. Suppiluliuma grew angry. A few years earlier, the Egyptians had attacked the city of Qadesh, part of his territory, and he had responded with similar violence. The Egyptians had initiated this mistrust between the two kingdoms. How could he know that his son would be safe?

Suspicion – the sense of a brewing conspiracy around every palace doorway – probably came easy to Suppiluliuma; he had only come to power because the Hittite elite turned on his brother, king for only a short time, and murdered him.[48] He considered his options, weighing up the possibilities. Was the prize of a united empire worth the risk to one of his sons' lives? Eventually, Hattusaziti's and Hani's accounts of events at the Egyptian royal court convinced him that there was no subterfuge. He cast aside his doubts and sent a prince to Egypt – his fourth son, Zannanza.

After preparing himself for the trip, the prince rode down from the high citadel of Hattusa and out of the city, nervous, excited, proud – it wasn't every day that someone invited you to be pharaoh. How might he adapt to his new surroundings and the requirements of Egyptian kingship? How much of his own Hittite beliefs could he merge with Egypt's traditions? Would he get along with his new wife? When he turned to see Hattusa one last time, he saw a city under construction, literally rising from the ashes, following a devastating attack and fire fifty years earlier.[49] How might it appear whenever he next returned? Zannanza and his entourage travelled south, eventually leaving Hittite territory. At some point along the way, they joined an Egyptian escort.[50] It would not be long before he would find himself in a new life in a new empire.

Zannanza did not survive the journey.

To Suppiluliuma, Egypt had committed murder. It was an act of war. After exchanging some letters with the Egyptians, giving them the chance to explain what had happened – they denied any guilt – he launched a campaign into Egyptian controlled-territory in the Levant.[51] This had an unintended consequence: his army contracted a plague and took it back to the Hittite homeland.[52]

Ankhesenamun's plan had failed. The death of the Hittite prince meant that another man would have to become Egypt's king, and with little time left to waste, this role fell to the elderly Aye. A single ring marks Aye's marriage to Ankhesenamun, though he would never mention her on his monuments. With the succession solved, the final preparations for Tutankhamun's burial could now begin. The king's mummy was ready, but the royal artisans hadn't yet finished decorating his tomb walls. The royal funeral was set for the end of March, a full seven months after Tutankhamun's death.

PAINTING TUTANKHAMUN'S TOMB

Painting by lamplight in Tutankhamun's burial chamber, the artisans worked in two teams on separate halves of the room. They painted a yellow background and then a grid, which helped them to transfer their designs from papyrus to the walls on a much larger scale – these designs had been carefully planned to meet the king's ritual requirements and ensure his afterlife existence. For the three walls decorated at this time, the artists used proportions introduced under Akhenaten, giving them a definite Amarna flavour.[53]

The artists decorated the east wall with a scene from the royal funeral, including a row of nobles dragging a sled bearing Tutankhamun's coffin.[54] On the north wall, they painted Aye performing the opening of the mouth ceremony on the boy king's mummy; as the crown prince normally led this ritual, it emphasized his legitimacy as successor. Aye perhaps requested inclusion of the scene close to the time of the funeral, or had it adapted for him following Zannanza's death, because the royal artisans painted it at high speed, carelessly leaving splatters of red and yellow paint on the wall.[55] To its left, there was Tutankhamun with the goddess Nut, and further along, Tutankhamun and Osiris embracing each other, watched by the king's ka-spirit. On the west wall – the direction of death – the artists painted select scenes from the *Book of What is in the Duat*, or *Amduat*, a royal underworld book, meant to ensure the king's success in the afterlife. Twelve baboons represented the twelve hours of the night, while above them were divinities and the solar boat. Unlike other royal tombs, the ceiling was left unpainted.[56]

Because the south wall, separating the burial chamber from the antechamber, had not yet been erected, the artisans had to wait until after the funeral and the installation of the burial equipment, to finish their work.[57] In the meantime, servants brought Tutankhamun's sarcophagus from the royal workshop to install it in the burial chamber, but found that they couldn't take it into the tomb until workmen widened the doorways and removed some of the steps.[58]

While the workmen manoeuvred the royal sarcophagus into position, members of the palace kitchen staff prepared food and drink for the funerary rituals and burial – goods that would sustain the king in the afterlife. They packed forty-eight boxes of meat – duck breast and wings, ox meat and geese – and baskets of chickpeas, fenugreek, lentils, peas, spices and almonds. There were bread and cake, emmer wheat and barley too,[59] and jars of honey and oils.[60] Perhaps due to their haste, the food they put in the boxes rarely matched the content lists written on the sides.[61] For drinks, the royal vintners sent a selection of wine: red wine, white wine and shedeh, as well as fruit juice.[62] One jar of wine was produced in the thirty-first year of King Amenhotep III's reign, forty years before Tutankhamun's death.[63] Some of the bread was meant for brewing beer with the help of strainers, which the kitchen staff included with the grave goods.[64] Other servants picked flowers to make funerary garlands,[65] which would be left in the tomb with the other treasures. Meanwhile, the royal artisans had been busy preparing bows and arrows for the burial, but with no time left, they had to send them to the tomb unfinished.[66] With these final preparations, the stage was finally set for Tutankhamun's long-delayed funeral.

THE ROYAL FUNERAL

Where the green fields meet the desert's edge on the west bank of the Nile at Thebes, Horemheb[67] and Aye, together with Egypt's two viziers and other high officials, stood in a line, gripping ropes ready to drag Tutankhamun's coffin on a sled. It was the day of the royal funeral, and before the king could be laid to rest in his tomb, they first had to take him from the embalming tent near his mortuary temple to various kiosks, where priests would perform rituals, either before Tutankhamun's mummy or before statues representing him. As the procession walked, priests burned incense and poured milk on the ground for the king. Priestesses performed the roles of the mourning goddesses Isis and Nephthys,[68] with Isis perhaps played by Ankhesenamun herself.[69] At each kiosk, Tutankhamun received offerings of various kinds – meats, wine, beer, bread – all piled on low tables.[70] After he magically devoured these offerings, mourners smashed the vessels that had contained them. Servants collected the

24. The mummy of Tutankhamun stands upright, while his successor, King Aye, performs the opening of the mouth ritual. Painted on a wall within Tutankhamun's burial chamber.

pottery fragments and any bones left over from the meat (in reality, eaten by the participants), put them in large vessels, and carried them in the funerary procession.[71] They joined other servants bearing the treasures to be buried in Tutankhamun's tomb. As the hours passed, the procession walked across the cultivation, and into the desert, where they took a path leading up the Theban hills to the Valley of the Kings.

Once the mourners arrived at the entrance to Tutankhamun's tomb, they watched the most important ritual of the funeral: the opening of the mouth ceremony. This was normally performed by the eldest son and successor – the next king – but in Tutankhamun's case, this role fell to Aye. Tutankhamun's mummy was raised up and made to stand before the mourners. Aye, a leopard skin draped over his shoulder, stepped forward and used a ritual adze to touch the king's mouth. This reactivated Tutankhamun's ability to speak in the afterlife,[72] and so proclaim that he had lived a just life when judged by the gods.

25. Tutankhamun's innermost coffin was made of solid gold.

The priests then carried Tutankhamun's body down his tomb's entrance corridor, through the antechamber and into the burial chamber. Along the way, they either dropped the body, or it fell over during one of the rituals, damaging his mask.[73] Next, they lowered him into the innermost of his three nested coffins in his sarcophagus. This coffin had been crafted entirely from gold, and when its lid was put in place, the workmen locked it with silver pins. They draped a linen shroud over the length of the coffin, poured liquid resin over it, and placed a garland of flowers over the vulture and cobra at the king's brow.[74] The middle and outermost coffins were sealed in turn.

FINALIZING THE BURIAL

Whenever convenient – either before the funeral or after, so as not to get in the way of the rituals – servants solemnly brought Tutankhamun's treasures into the tomb and placed them in the chambers. They put Tutankhamun's canopic chest in the treasury,[75] rather than close to his body in the burial chamber. It was hidden within a canopic shrine of gilded wood, with each side protected by a different goddess: Selket, Isis, Neith and Nephthys.[76] A golden shrine, decorated with images of Tutankhamun and Ankhesenamun, was placed in the antechamber,[77] and a statue of Anubis as a jackal, lying on a shrine, was left in the treasury.[78] Servants tied a sash around the jackal's neck and draped it with a striped linen tunic from the reign of Akhenaten.[79] The shrine beneath was filled with items used during Tutankhamun's mummification.[80] Behind the jackal, they placed a wooden cow head with copper horns, and wrapped linen around its neck.[81] This represented the goddess Mehet-Weret, a celestial cow and creator goddess, who in some myths was the mother of the sun god Re.[82]

26. Tutankhamun's canopic shrine. Each side
is protected by a different goddess.

27. The jackal on this shrine represents the god Anubis.

With the king now resting in his sarcophagus, the time had come to lift its lid into position. The workmen raised its heavy weight – and froze. There was a cracking sound. It was breaking. To quickly repair the lid, they mixed powdered limestone with resin and used it as a glue to reconnect the two pieces. Then – so that no one would ever know what had happened – they painted over the crack.[83] Once they'd lowered the lid, another problem arose: the outermost coffin's feet didn't quite fit. The lid jutted open. The artisans set to work again, this time filing down the feet so that the lid sealed properly.[84] Meanwhile, priests placed figurines of Osiris, Anubis, a djed-pillar (a symbol of Osiris) and a human-headed mummy into four niches cut into the burial chamber walls, each standing on a 'magic brick'. When installing them, the priests didn't properly follow the instructions given in the Book of the Dead, a collection of spells that helped the deceased to successfully navigate the afterlife realm and pass judgement; the Osiris figurine wasn't necessary, and it replaced the traditional torch brick, which was placed in the treasury instead. Close enough was apparently good enough. Afterwards, workmen sealed, plastered and painted over the niches, though the shade of yellow they used didn't quite match the earlier paint.[85] It appears that everyone was in a hurry to go home.

Next, the workmen started constructing four nested shrines that enclosed the sarcophagus. Bringing them into the burial chamber had already caused a headache – despite being deconstructed into separate panels, they still didn't fit, so the workmen had to remove a piece of the chamber's wall just to get them inside.[86] Now within, they still had to be fitted together, a job made all the more difficult by the limited space and light. Working fast, the workmen banged the panels together, damaging the gilded decoration and leaving wooden splinters on the floor. They followed instructions written on the panels' sides, but even so, because of their haste, they built the shrines the wrong way around from what had been intended. The sides meant to face west, faced east, and so forth.[87] As the shrines came together, priests placed ritual items on the floor in the small spaces between them. So, after the workmen had built the innermost shrine around the sarcophagus, the priests laid down bows, arrows and two fans, each bearing feathers of brown and white. These were hidden from view when the workmen constructed the next shrine in the sequence.[88] Around the second to last shrine, they erected a wooden frame and draped a linen pall over it.[89]

While this was happening, other craftsmen were busy building a wall between the burial chamber and the antechamber, in which they'd leave a doorway just big enough for people to move between the two rooms.[90] Once this was raised, artists decorated the side of the wall inside the burial chamber. They painted three seated gods, identified as lords of the Duat (the afterlife realm), and Tutankhamun in the presence of Isis, Anubis and Hathor, who offers the ankh-symbol of life to the king's lips.[91] When laying out these scenes, the artists followed Egypt's traditional grid proportions, making them appear less influenced by Amarna art than the paintings on the other walls.[92] When the last artists left the burial chamber through the doorway in the newly-built wall, ready for it to be sealed behind them, they left two lamps alight,[93] illuminating the room for just a little while longer. Then, when the remaining grave goods had been placed inside the other chambers, the workmen laid stones in the tomb's entrance doorway, blocking it. They covered it with a layer of plaster and, before it dried, necropolis officials stamped it with their seals.[94] This marked the formal closure of the tomb. The only thing left to do was to bury the items used during Tutankhamun's mummification and funerary rituals in a nearby pit.[95]

28. Seals stamped by necropolis officials on the wall that separated Tutankhamun's antechamber from the burial chamber.

And so, with the flickering lights of the torches burning to their last breath, darkness fell within the tomb. Within his coffin, Tutankhamun stared upwards, towards the sky, where his spirit could fully, finally, become embroiled in the eternal struggle for maat – cosmic order, justice and balance.

He had achieved his ultimate destiny.

Each time the sun rose in the morning, shimmering on the horizon, it meant that Tutankhamun had succeeded in helping the sun god defeat his enemies. Maat was sustained and the world would continue. The months-long efforts of Ankhesenamun, courtiers, embalmers, priests and artisans to guarantee the king's survival in the afterlife were worth it. Nonetheless, tomb robbers or a royal successor who might want to eradicate Tutankhamun and his Amarna family from memory would pose an ongoing potential threat. If his name, mummy or tomb treasures were lost or destroyed, he could still be wiped from existence, and lose his role in the cosmic cycle of rebirth.

Tutankhamun was dead, yet alive. But the danger of a second death remained.

5

The Dark Before the Dawn

It had been quite a ride for Aye – now officially King Aye. He had progressed from true believer in Akhenaten's regime, to prominent royal adviser and convert to the traditional ways, to pharaoh. He can't have predicted this future for himself. No one could. Although he had been close to the royal family for his entire career, and his marriage to Ankhesenamun had helped to legitimize his newfound position, Aye pushed the widowed queen into the background – Aye's Great Royal Wife was Tiye, his wife since at least his Amarna days, and she would be the most prominent woman at his court. Yet Ankhesenamun's shadow loomed large, at least initially. After Aye's coronation, he tried to defuse the situation with the Hittites created by the death of Zannanza, Ankhesenamun's doomed fiancé. In a letter written to Suppiluliuma, Aye mentioned the prince's death and his hope that peaceful relations could exist between the two kingdoms. It got him nowhere. The Hittite king believed that Egypt had murdered his son, and continued to attack Egyptian territory in the northern Levant.[1] Given the ongoing problems between the two kingdoms since the reign of Akhenaten, this was nothing new, so Aye turned his attention to more pressing matters at home.

Just as under Tutankhamun, construction would be a theme of Aye's reign. He sent his workmen to finish building one of Tutankhamun's Theban temples, and began new temples elsewhere around the country, particularly in his home town of Akhmim,[2] where people worshipped the fertility god Min. But destruction would also be a theme. During his first year as king, Aye's workmen reopened the small tomb in the Valley of the Kings in which Tutankhamun had interred members of his Amarna family and some of their burial equipment. Within, they defaced Akhenaten's coffin, obliterating the king's name wherever it was found and breaking away its gilded face, leaving only its vague shape in the wood. Whatever kindness Tutankhamun had shown to his heretic father with this reburial, it was stripped away by Aye's vandals. This wasn't an isolated incident. Akhenaten's name was removed from monuments across the country. His obliteration from memory had fully begun.[3]

TOMB ROBBERY

Within Tutankhamun's tomb, there was the muffled sound of chiselling. It could be heard coming from the entrance corridor outside, but grew slowly nearer and nearer. Suddenly, plaster crumbled and stone fell. A sliver of light from a burning wick illuminated a pair of eyes. A man peered through the gap into the antechamber – he could see wonderful things. Behind him, there were others, each just as eager to get inside the tomb and see what they could take. Earlier, by cover of night, the thieves had pierced the tomb's first doorway and sneaked along the descending corridor. To reach deeper inside, all it took was for them to force an opening in the upper-left section of the second doorway, breaking through the plaster and rubble that sealed it. Crawling through the gap and dropping to the antechamber's floor, all of Tutankhamun's treasures lay before them.

Not knowing how much time they had, the thieves worked quickly, grabbing whatever they could fit through their forced entrance to resell as soon as possible. Anything they took must not be traceable back to the tomb.[4] They rifled through boxes, grabbing jars filled with sweet-smelling unguents, the contents so fresh that they'd easily find a buyer. One thief dipped his fingers into a cosmetics vessel, leaving his mark for thousands of years.[5] Others took metal vessels, which they could melt down and recast. The thieves stood on boxes, leaving their footprints behind, and crawled beneath the ritual couch of the goddess Ammit to force their way through the blocked doorway beneath, which separated the antechamber from the annexe.[6] Within, they opened boxes and rummaged through the other treasures. As they fled the tomb, they dropped some of their plunder, leaving behind pieces of gilded wood and gold, and bronze items, including an arrowhead.[7]

Tomb robbery was not unusual in ancient Egypt. The thieves who broke into Tutankhamun's tomb were following a tradition that stretched back to the earliest days of their civilization. With the recent upheavals in society, the valley's security had not yet returned to its earlier level of protection, leaving gaps of opportunity. Plus, the thieves were probably the same people who helped to bury Tutankhamun in the first place[8] – people who knew the tomb's layout, its location, how it had been sealed, and the extent of its riches. They would also have been aware of the punishments if they were caught: a short imprisonment, torture and interrogation, then execution, most likely by impalement.

When the authorities discovered the break-in at Tutankhamun's tomb, they restored a certain order to the treasures. They didn't replace any of the stolen items though, and some of the disturbed objects were returned to the wrong boxes, despite the labels clearly listing their original contents.[9] They left the doorway between the annexe and the antechamber broken, picked up the items dropped by the tomb robbers, placed them in the entrance corridor and resealed the entrance, stamping their official seals in the wet plaster to mark their inspection. To make it harder to break into the tomb, the necropolis officials asked the workmen to fill the entrance corridor with stone chippings, which buried the objects left there. Clearly, no one had much interest in spending time tidying the tomb – seal it quickly and move on was probably the directive. After all, the Deir el-Medina artisans were meant to be preparing Aye's tomb in the western valley, not wasting work days on Tutankhamun.

Shortly afterwards, a second group of thieves arrived at Tutankhamun's tomb.[10] Over the course of about seven hours they breached its entrance and forced a tunnel through the barrier of chippings, emptying the rubble outside. They clearly weren't in a rush. Once inside, they ransacked the antechamber and annexe, and broke through into the burial chamber, giving them access to the treasury. As they searched through the treasures, they opened the royal chests and stole jewellery, wrapping gold rings in linen to make them easier to carry.[11] Although the thieves possibly entered the tomb on multiple occasions, in the end, their luck ran out. The valley guards caught them in the act and returned their final spoils to the tomb. The thieves would surely have been executed soon after. It again fell to the necropolis authorities to swiftly put the tomb back in order, reseal the doorways and refill the chippings in the entrance corridor. Among the staff was a man named Djehutymose who, while working in the annexe, took the opportunity to write his name on a jar, perhaps expecting that no one would ever notice.[12]

Not long after the tomb had been resealed, a storm erupted over the Valley of the Kings. Within moments, a few rare drops of rain had transformed into a downpour. Lightning cracked the sky and thunder roared – to the Egyptians, a phenomenon caused by the god Seth. Growing deeper and deeper, the water slid along the desert plateau and into the great channels of the Valley of the Kings.[13] It crashed through these channels, now around two metres deep, picking up rubble as it moved, transforming the dry desert paths into a network of rivers. These rivers converged on the central Valley of the Kings, right at the location of Tutankhamun's tomb. Hours later, when the rain stopped and the water dissipated, the tomb's entrance lay sealed beneath about a metre of hard rubble.[14] If Tutankhamun hadn't yet fully reached the underworld, he certainly had now.

It had only been a year since his burial.

THE DEATH AND BURIAL OF KING AYE

Horemheb probably felt a sense of déjà vu when he heard that Aye had died. Aye was an old man, and his death was not unexpected like that of Tutankhamun, but his reign had been short, only four years, and there was no complete tomb for him to be buried within. Aye also lacked an obvious successor, because his son, General Nakhtmin, had recently died.[15] With Ankhesenamun out of the picture, and no other surviving member of the royal line, even a tangential one, stepping forward, the kingship would have to pass to a courtier. As deputy of the king under Tutankhamun, a position even higher than the vizier, Horemheb was the obvious option.

Once again, the artisans of Deir el-Medina mobilized at high speed to finalize a burial in time for a king's funeral. They were used to this by now, but the situation wasn't as dire as under Tutankhamun. Aye had founded his mortuary temple early in his reign, so it was already under construction, and he had appropriated the tomb in the Valley of the Kings originally meant for Tutankhamun – this was fitting, given that the boy king had been buried in his tomb. No work had begun from scratch; nonetheless, the craftsmen didn't transform Aye's tomb into an elaborate burial place. They took what existed and – as in Tutankhamun's tomb – focused their attention on decorating the burial chamber. They dedicated one wall to the first hour of the *Book of What is in the Duat*, a time when the sun god – and by extension, the dead king – was believed to enter the underworld; another wall to Aye in the presence of the gods; and another to the Book of the Dead. Elsewhere, they painted Aye and his wife, Queen Tiye, hunting in the marshes – a scene common in private tombs, but not in the tombs of kings.[16]

29. The burial chamber of King Aye, in his tomb in the western part of the Valley of the Kings.

Little can be said about Aye's funeral, but as it was Horemheb who succeeded him, he surely conducted the mortuary rituals, including the opening of the mouth ceremony, just as Aye had done for Tutankhamun. But unlike Aye with Tutankhamun, Horemheb put little effort into assembling a lavish burial for his predecessor – his tomb only contained a small number of items.[17] There's a sense that everybody wanted this brief phase to be over and done with. When Horemheb oversaw the door to Aye's tomb being blocked with stones and stamped with the seals of the necropolis, he can't have been nostalgic for the past. He swiftly moved on to considering his own reign, and how he could right the wrongs that his predecessors had inflicted on the country that he'd spent his entire life fighting for.

THE STORY OF HOREMHEB

When Horemheb ascended the throne, he'd earned it. He'd fought wars in the south and east for Akhenaten and Tutankhamun. He'd watched a new religious movement erupt and then collapse, and steered the country in its aftermath. He'd witnessed a dynasty die. Now, he, even more of a commoner than Aye, was about to become king. To legitimize this move would take some clever messaging. Horemheb's prestige at court, military successes, and elevation to king's deputy had already cemented his high position, but to be king required the approval of the gods, not just the court. The pharaoh served as intermediary between the human and the divine, it wasn't simply another office to add to his long string of official titles. For Horemheb to truly become pharaoh, he needed a suitably grand story, so he asked his scribes to write a coronation inscription for him, one that explained his rise and connections to the divine. It was distributed across the country, inscribed on royal stelae and statues, and probably read aloud to gathered crowds.

The story began with Horemheb's birth – he was thorough – when he already appeared god-like and those who saw him offered him their praises.[18] Horemheb was a child of the falcon god Horus, the story goes, but the god wanted him to have a career before revealing his true destiny to the world. Horemheb rose to the top of the administration, and whenever discussions in the palace collapsed into arguments, he stepped in, watched by the king, to calm everyone down. Once Horemheb had built a successful career, Horus decided it was time for him to visit Thebes, where he would become king. During the Opet Festival, having walked through the Colonnade Hall of Luxor Temple, past images of Tutankhamun and Ankhesenamun, Horemheb stood before Amun and was crowned by the god. He then set out to restore the temples and make new divine statues – much as Tutankhamun had done, but without any acknowledgement of his predecessor's efforts.

30. A statue of King Horemheb and the falcon-headed god Horus.

Horemheb inherited an Egypt with much the same issues that Tutankhamun and Aye had faced: a religious establishment that needed restoring and an empire under threat from the Hittites. But although he had dedicated much of his career to the military, and travelled widely across Egypt's empire, it was reforms at home that mainly preoccupied his kingship. To cement his control, Horemheb installed judges across the country, chosen by himself, and sought to punish officials who abused their positions, such as those who took goods meant for the palace or who overtaxed the people of Egypt. He also set new punishments for soldiers caught stealing,[19] perhaps something that he'd witnessed himself. The sentences for those found breaking his new laws could be extreme – exile was among them, as was mutilation of the offender's face, leaving a permanent sign to all around that this person had offended the pharaoh. He also appointed new high priests, selected from among the military ranks.[20] On the world stage, Horemheb launched campaigns into Nubia and the Levant, his troops returning to Egypt with prisoners, and he traded with the land of Punt.[21]

Meanwhile, the craftsmen of Deir el-Medina set to work digging a royal tomb for Horemheb in the Valley of the Kings. For the first time in years, this would be a completely new project, descending into untouched earth. When the chambers and corridors had been carved from the rock, Horemheb demanded that his artisans create finer decoration than had been produced for his predecessors' tombs, so instead of just painting the scenes, they painstakingly carved them first.[22] At the same time, artisans in the royal workshops crafted the ritual items that Horemheb needed to achieve his afterlife, including a red granite sarcophagus.[23]

Now that he was king, Horemheb no longer needed the large and lavish tomb that he'd constructed over the years at

Saqqara. Nonetheless, he still sent artisans to the necropolis to add a royal uraeus – the rearing cobra worn at the brow of pharaohs – to all carvings of him.[24] Keeping the tomb up-to-date was clearly important to Horemheb; it was already the burial place of a prominent woman in his life, one who had perhaps been his first wife.[25] And years later, he returned to the tomb to bury his Great Royal Wife, Queen Mutnodjmet, who probably died during childbirth.[26]

THE DESTRUCTION OF TUTANKHAMUN AND AYE

Though Horemheb had lived through the reigns of Akhenaten, Tutankhamun and Aye, he no longer regarded them as true kings, worthy of being remembered. It was better for Egypt to bury their memory, he decided. Wherever his artisans travelled in Egypt, they usurped monuments, chiselling out the names of his immediate predecessors and replacing them with his own. Not only would this cause later generations to forget that they had ever lived, but the removal of their names meant obliteration from existence. If Horemheb had succeeded in his mission, he would have caused these pharaohs to vanish from the afterlife – a second death from which there was no return. Even for a general accustomed to the brutality of war, this was rather extreme.

During this campaign of destruction, Horemheb's men entered Aye's tomb and hacked away the images of Aye and Tiye, along with their names. They pushed off his sarcophagus lid, and perhaps even robbed some of his grave goods and destroyed his mummy.[27] Horemheb then completed work on Aye's mortuary temple, but replaced all of the names with his own.[28] At Karnak, the target was Tutankhamun's Restoration Stele, on which every reference to the boy king was changed into Horemheb, making it appear that he was responsible for the return to tradition after Akhenaten. His men removed two carvings of Ankhesenamun too, leaving Horemheb standing alone in the presence of the gods.[29] At nearby Luxor Temple, scaffolding was re-erected so workmen could remove Tutankhamun's names from his grand carvings of the Opet Festival in the Colonnade Hall.[30] Across Egypt, Horemheb usurped Tutankhamun's newly-crafted statues, something that Aye had not done;[31] perhaps Aye had a higher level of respect for the young king.

The one place that Horemheb's vandals couldn't reach was Tutankhamun's tomb. Horemheb and the artisans of Deir el-Medina knew its location, of course, but with it cut off from the world beneath a hard layer of flood debris, it would have taken them an impressive amount of effort to break through the ground to reach its entrance – effort that the workmen clearly had no interest in expending.

BORN OF RE

As the years of Horemheb's reign passed, familiar problems reappeared. The king had no surviving children, and without a clear successor, Egypt risked descending into chaos. Horemheb's solution was to turn to a trusted ex-military official. Paramessu probably started his career around the time of Horemheb's coronation and quickly ascended the military ranks, passing from troop commander into the chariotry, and then becoming a diplomatic envoy. After periods as a general and overseer of a border fortress, his standing at court was such that Horemheb appointed him vizier. His years of experience in the military, diplomatic and government spheres, plus having the ear of the king, made him the perfect candidate to become pharaoh. To ensure that this happened, Horemheb elevated Paramessu further, making him king's deputy.

Horemheb's appointment of Paramessu – the future King Ramesses I – as royal successor changed the course of Egypt's history. A new phase began – a clean break. And because Paramessu already had both an adult son and grandson – the man who would one day be known as Ramesses the Great – Egypt's future stability was assured.[32] After Horemheb's death, these kings continued the eradication of the Amarna pharaohs and dismantled their monuments, whilst restoring the name of Amun wherever they found it destroyed.

Through all of this, Tutankhamun remained safely sealed in his tomb, but with his name removed from temple walls and king lists, and his family dead, the memory of him began to fade. Many years later, when artisans were busy preparing the tomb of King Ramesses VI, they built their work huts above Tutankhamun's tomb entrance, unaware that he rested just a metre below.

Tutankhamun's tomb remained untouched when a new wave of thieves entered the Valley of the Kings, two hundred years after his burial, and later, when priests transferred the royal mummies to hiding places, keeping their treasures for themselves. He lay undisturbed, preserved in the darkness, through the rise of great empires – the Assyrians, Babylonians, Persians, Macedonian-Greeks and Romans – and their control of Egypt, and into the era of Coptic Christianity and Islam. While he rested, Ashurbanipal, Alexander the Great, Cleopatra, Julius Caesar, Amr Ibn El-as, Saladin and Mohammed Ali lived and died, unaware of his existence.

Eventually though, Tutankhamun did see the light of day again, reborn as a celebrity in a world he could never have imagined.

6

The Lost Tomb

By the late nineteenth and early twentieth centuries, Egypt had become a tourist magnet. People arrived in Luxor by steamer or train from Cairo, and stayed in grand hotels along the Nile. One favourite was the elegant Winter Palace Hotel, a stone's throw from Luxor Temple.[1] Men in three-piece suits and women in pale dresses and wide hats explored the romantic ruins of the Nile's east bank, or they crossed the river by ferry to visit the remains of royal mortuary temples and crumbling tombs. They left early in the morning to avoid the heat, transported by donkeys or carriages ordered a day in advance, and with lunches packed in baskets by hotel staff.[2] When they arrived in the Valley of the Kings they found some of the royal tombs fitted with electric lighting – an initiative led by a certain antiquities inspector called Howard Carter (though they were only switched on from November to March between 9 a.m. and 1 p.m.).[3] If tourists could get the key from the local chief inspector, they could add to their itinerary a visit to the tomb of an official named Huy, who served under a little-known king named 'Tut-enkh-Amun'.[4]

Amidst all this, the Egyptians tried to get on with their lives. Luxor was booming, but its people were the backdrop to the Westerners' exciting adventures of discovery – disregarded as little more than assistants to sun-drenched dreams. Egyptians were a backdrop to political life too. From 1882, while technically still part of the Ottoman Empire, Egypt was a 'veiled' British protectorate – the latest foreign occupation in a long list that stretched back into ancient times. The antiquities service, guardian of Egypt's monuments, had been under foreign control from before that time; it had been dominated by Western, and particularly French, scholars since 1858, when the French archaeologist Auguste Mariette became its director.[5] Laws to protect Egypt's heritage had been established in 1835, but in the early twentieth century, it was still normal for foreign excavations to keep half of what they discovered, so long as the artefacts exported were similar enough to ones already in Egypt. This was good business for rich collectors and museums, but not good for Egypt, which was being bled dry of its heritage.

CARTER AND CARNARVON

The discovery of Tutankhamun's tomb was the result of the collision of two very different lives. Born in Brompton, London, on 9 May 1874,[6] Howard Carter first travelled to Egypt when he was seventeen,[7] having taken a job as an artist, copying scenes from tomb walls for academic publications. He then studied excavation techniques at Amarna, neatly foreshadowing his future association with Tutankhamun.[8] Eventually, he joined Egypt's antiquities service as an inspector, initially working at Luxor, and afterwards in the office that managed the north and middle of Egypt. He was based at Saqqara, a necropolis that had become popular with tourists thanks to its pyramids and painted tombs, and its easy access from Cairo. It was there, at the Serapeum, burial place of the sacred Apis bulls, that a dispute between a group of French tourists and antiquities guards escalated and threatened Carter's career.

According to one version of events, the tourists had no tickets, but wanted to see inside the Serapeum. Tensions grew, and eventually one of the tourists hit a guard. When Carter arrived, he argued with the group. Then a guard hit one of the tourists. After the tourists complained to the French Consul-General, Carter was ordered to apologize. He refused, saying that he'd only apologize once the French visitors had done so. Carter wouldn't budge, so there was little that the antiquities service could do, but reassign him. After a short spell as chief inspector

31. Howard Carter (right) and Lord Carnarvon (left) in March 1923.

for Lower Egypt, based in Tanta in the Delta, he resigned in 1905. Carter moved to Luxor and made a living as an artist. It would be three years until he met Lord Carnarvon, changing the direction of his life.[9]

Carnarvon had quite a different journey. Born on 26 June 1866, educated in a private school, and then at Eton and Cambridge University, he was famously generous and enjoyed a life of watching horse racing, sailing and golf. But perhaps most important to his future fate, he developed an interest in cars – an interest that would nearly kill him. One day, speeding along a German road, Carnarvon flipped his car. It landed on top of him. His heart stopped. And although he survived, he never fully recovered. Warned that his health could deteriorate during the cold and wet British winters, he decided to spend these months in Egypt, staying at the appropriately titled Winter Palace Hotel, which was closed during the hot summer months.[10] He may not have expected to end up here, but Carnarvon had long been fascinated by archaeology and excavation, and now found himself in the perfect place to explore his interest.[11]

In 1906, through a connection in Egypt, Carnarvon secured the right to excavate at Qurna in Luxor, the location of the ancient tombs of the nobles. Without any experience, he directed his first excavation season in 1907. After two seasons,[12] there were limited results, but his enthusiasm hadn't dampened. To bring in some extra expertise, Gaston Maspero, head of the antiquities service, recommended that Carnarvon work with Howard Carter.[13] They began their collaboration in 1909. Over the following years, the archaeologist and his sponsor excavated at Thebes, the Delta sites of Sakha and Tell el-Balamun, and ultimately gained the concession to work in the Valley of the Kings – a dream come true for both, but badly timed.

When the First World War erupted in 1914, Egypt became an official British protectorate. The 'veiled' approach was dropped. Carnarvon was prevented from travelling to Egypt, and Carter, in Egypt, had little time to dedicate towards archaeology, beyond some work in the royal tombs of Amenhotep III and Hatshepsut.[14] They put their plans on hold, but Carter still spent time poring over a map he'd made of the Valley of the Kings, searching for any area that had not yet been properly investigated.[15]

One tomb in particular was on his mind.

Over the years, Carter had collected evidence that Tutankhamun's tomb lay hidden somewhere in the Valley of the Kings.[16] He noted that in 1907, excavations in the valley had revealed a small pit filled with items from Tutankhamun's reign, among them, linen, floral collars and broken pots stored in jars.[17] A later examination suggested that these were the remains of Tutankhamun's funeral. He knew that in 1909, gold foil naming Tutankhamun and Ankhesenamun had been found in a small chamber in the valley,[18] and close by, beneath a rock, there had been a faience cup bearing the king's name. Its excavators declared this simple chamber to be Tutankhamun's tomb, ending the mystery of its where-abouts,[19] but Carter suspected otherwise. Crucially, these finds were all made in the same little-explored area of the central valley, Carter noticed, the same place that the tomb contain-ing Tutankhamun's reburied Amarna royal family had been found in 1907.[20] It was clear to Carter that this was a hub of burials from Tutankhamun's reign[21] – the exact place that you'd expect the king's tomb to be found. It was a tempting thought – the stuff of quests.

Because of the war, Carter and Carnarvon's search for the tomb of Tutankhamun only truly began in 1917. Placing all of their effort in the under-explored triangle identified by Carter, they spent five seasons with little to show for it. Each winter, Carter travelled to Egypt to oversee the excavation, and the Egyptian workmen hauled away huge amounts of rubble, digging their way down to the bedrock. Dig, haul, repeat. Dig, haul, repeat. Dig, haul, repeat.

After five seasons, Carter at least knew where ancient tombs weren't located.

In 1922, Carnarvon asked Carter to visit him at Highclere Castle, his home in Hampshire, in England. Enough was enough. Fifteen years of funding excavations in Egypt had cost him around £40,000 to £50,000, the equivalent of millions today.[22] He owned a castle, but he wasn't made of money. It was time to stop. But Carter had other plans: during their first season, they had identified a patch of land beneath some workmen's huts that had seemed promising. He wanted to excavate there, he said, even if it meant funding it himself. Carnarvon was won over by Carter's enthusiasm, and offered to pay for one final season. It was one more for the road.[23] One last shot.

THE DISCOVERY

The work began on 1 November 1922, a Wednesday. Carter's team started by excavating and recording the workmen's huts from the reign of King Ramesses VI.[24] From that moment, things moved fast. On 4 November 1922, at 10 a.m., Carter's excavation team, led by their foreman Ahmed Gerigar, uncovered ancient steps, descending into the bedrock. In his pocket diary, Carter excitedly recorded the discovery diagonally across the page.[25] His team spent the rest of the day, and then the next day too, unearthing twelve steps, and eventually the upper part of a doorway which was stamped with the seals of the ancient necropolis. But who did this tomb belong to? Carter couldn't see a name.

Beneath the doorway's lintel, Carter forced a small opening. It was just big enough for him to insert an electric light and see inside. There was a corridor filled with rubble. It was a good sign that whatever lay beyond was intact – but the question remained, what did lie beyond? To Carter, it didn't appear like a royal tomb. He wondered whether it was made for an ancient courtier, or perhaps it was a cache – a place where mummification material was stored. At this stage, there was no indication that it belonged to a king, and certainly not to Tutankhamun. Nevertheless, that evening, Carter sent a message to Carnarvon in England: he'd found an intact tomb. He'd wait for his arrival before excavating further. Carter's team reburied the steps. It would be two weeks before Lord Carnarvon and his daughter Lady Evelyn disembarked in Egypt. News that a discovery had been made in the Valley of the Kings started to make its way around the country.

By 24 November, Carter and Carnarvon were together again in the Valley of the Kings, and the excavation resumed. The steps were uncovered, and they began to fully reveal the doorway. As they carefully cleared the rubble, dust and sand from the bottom of the door, there was a moment of excitement and relief. The seal imprints, pressed into its mud-plastered surface thousands of years earlier, bore a name: King Tutankhamun.

Carter had been right all along. He'd made history. Or had he?

Doubts about what remained inside the tomb still plagued Carter's mind. Along the stairway leading down to the door, the team had discovered broken pots bearing the names of Tutankhamun, Akhenaten and Smenkhkare. Other artefacts were dated to the reigns of Tuthmosis III and Amenhotep III. These finds once again raised the possibility that their discovery was a cache, not a tomb. Plus, it was clear that the doorway had been broken through in ancient times. Had the tomb – or whatever he had found – been robbed? Carter's fears only grew when his workmen removed the doorway's blocking stones and hauled away the rubble that filled the corridor beyond. In the upper left part of the corridor, a tunnel along its length had been filled with stones that differed from the rest. To Carter, there was only one conclusion: someone had tunnelled through, and their damage had been repaired. Artefacts scattered in the rubble, dropped perhaps, further indicated the presence of ancient thieves.

On 26 November, Carter's team finished clearing the entrance corridor. It led to another doorway, covered in stamped seals of the necropolis. It too had been pierced at some ancient time – whoever penetrated the corridor had entered the tomb. What would be left inside?

Carter, Carnarvon, Lady Evelyn, archaeologist Arthur Callender and the Egyptian foremen in charge of the excavation gathered in the cramped space at the end of the corridor. They watched as Carter made a small hole in the top left corner of the door and poked an iron rod through into the darkness. There was an empty space beyond. He removed a little more of the doorway, asked for a candle, and leaned inside. Everyone waited for news. The candle flickered. Carter glanced around. Illuminated before him was a treasure trove of ancient artefacts. He couldn't believe his eyes. Carnarvon was eager to learn what Carter could see. It must have felt like an eternity waiting for the archaeologist's response.

'Wonderful things,' Carter said.[26]

Carter expanded the hole so that Carnarvon could see for himself. An electric light brightened the space. Both archaeologist and sponsor must have felt a sense of wonder. In that small chamber, time had stopped. Despite all the signs of ancient thieves, it appeared almost totally intact. But one question still hadn't been resolved: was this truly the tomb of King Tutankhamun? Was he buried somewhere inside? Taking turns to peer through the hole in the doorway, the group didn't find the answer. The day ended, and they sealed the entrance with a wooden grille. Carter sent word to the chief inspector of the antiquities department: they had entered the tomb and made a great discovery.

32. The antechamber of Tutankhamun's tomb when it was first found by Howard Carter. The wall leading into the burial chamber is still blocked.

THE FIRST STEPS INSIDE

By noon the next day, Carter's team had dismantled the second doorway. For the first time, Carter, Carnarvon and Lady Evelyn could step among the treasures, later joined by Ibrahim Habib, an inspector from Luxor's department of antiquities. Treading carefully, they saw that the chamber had been left in a state of chaos. Objects lay broken or upside down, dumped and knocked over by ancient thieves. The officials who resealed the room had only done the bare minimum necessary to restore order. The group peered beneath a ritual couch carved with the head of a hippopotamus to find a small door, broken through by the tomb robbers. Carter and Carnarvon crawled beneath it into the annexe. Pieces of the doorway still lay on the objects, exactly where they'd fallen thousands of years before. Back in the antechamber, they spotted the tell-tale signs of a repaired breach in a wall and guessed that it might lead to the burial chamber. The thieves must have broken through that too – how much might remain inside?

The temptation to know proved too much.

Without recording the event in his notes and journal, Carter and the group allegedly reopened the hole and peered into the burial chamber. There were sighs of relief. The burial appeared intact. The cartouches of Tutankhamun were everywhere in the chambers they'd explored, and now they'd confirmed the presence of a burial chamber: it was definitely the king's tomb. Satisfied, they left, resealed the breach, and covered it over with reeds and a basket.[27]

On 29 November, Carter held an event to officially open the tomb, attended by local dignitaries, archaeologists and a reporter from the British newspaper, *The Times*. Over the following weeks, other archaeologists, dignitaries and journalists visited the tomb too. They were the first trickle that would eventually become a torrential flood. Meanwhile, Carter had to figure out how best to record and preserve Tutankhamun's treasures. On a week-long trip to Cairo in early December, he bought various supplies, including a steel gate to block the tomb's entrance, packing material, boxes, chemicals and bandages. He also bought a car. The grand Parisian-inspired boulevards and bustle of life in the great city must have felt a world away from his quiet mud-brick home on Luxor's west bank – 'Castle Carter' – just a short donkey ride from the Valley of the Kings.

The impact of his discovery, and the scale of the work ahead, weighed on Carter's mind. The tomb and its contents would take years to clear, to conserve, to record. Importantly, he decided that every artefact should be photographed, both as it was discovered in the tomb, and afterwards, as individual objects. Carter couldn't do this alone, so he reached out to the Metropolitan Museum of Art's expedition in Egypt and found them happy to send experts to join the project,[28] including their photographer, Harry Burton. Meanwhile, the conservation and restoration work would be led by Alfred Lucas, a chemist with the Egyptian government.[29] Just before Christmas, the team assembled in the Valley of the Kings. They used the tomb of King Seti II, known as KV 15, as their laboratory, and Lucas began testing chemicals to preserve the fragile artefacts.

Towards the end of December, just over a month after entering the tomb, Carter's team removed the first artefact from the antechamber: it was Tutankhamun's painted wooden chest, decorated with colourful scenes of the king riding on his chariot against enemies and hunting animals. Just as Carter did throughout the excavation, he assigned the chest a number: 21. This chest was also the first artefact to be conserved by Lucas.

Taking his brush, he carefully wiped away the dust of millennia. He filled bubbles of blistered paint with paraffin wax, and secured loose paint and cracks with a celluloid solution. This was not entirely successful – the changing temperatures and need to move the chest for photography led the paint over the joints to start peeling away. To solve this problem, Lucas placed plasticine in the cracks and covered the box in melted paraffin wax.[30] This was the first of thousands of artefacts that he would conserve over the following decade. As the weeks passed, and 1922 became 1923, the team systematically emptied the antechamber and their time was filled with meetings and research.

The day had come for Carter to remove the wall that separated the antechamber from the burial chamber before the eyes of assembled dignitaries.[31] It was 16 February 1923. The antechamber was now empty, except for the guests' chairs, two 'guardian' statues and a wooden platform, erected against the wall, which hid the earlier sealed breach and gave Carter access to its top. Carnarvon and Carter gave speeches, and Carter then began to dismantle the wall, assisted by archaeologist Arthur Mace.[32] As the guests looked on and took photos, he eventually made enough space to lean inside. With the help of an electric light, he illuminated the outermost golden shrine.[33] Gold reflected back on the faces of the onlookers. It was finally clear to everyone that Carter had discovered an intact tomb.

Within those shrines, Tutankhamun surely still lay inside his sarcophagus.

Ten days later, the excavation phase of the season ended and Carter resealed the tomb. Research and conservation work continued on the treasures in the 'laboratory', while Harry Burton used tomb KV 55 – where Tutankhamun had reburied his Amarna family – as his darkroom, developing photos that would cause the world's first wave of Tut-mania.

33. Howard Carter (right) and Arthur Callender (left) wrapping a guardian statue. One of the shrines surrounding Tutankhamun's sarcophagus can be seen in the burial chamber behind them.

DEALING WITH THE MEDIA

After news of the discovery broke, everyone wanted the latest updates. Journalists tried to secure interviews with Carter and visit the tomb, and tourists sat outside, waiting to see what mysterious artefacts might appear from the dark corridor leading into the ground. The world, however, learned of the latest developments through newspapers. Shortly after the tomb's discovery, Carnarvon made a deal with the British newspaper,

The Times. Their reporter had already been the sole journalist present at the tomb's official opening,[34] but this deal went further, assigning *The Times* exclusive rights to the ongoing story of the tomb's excavation. *The Times* would receive an update each evening direct from the tomb,[35] and could sell their stories and images to other news outlets the world over.[36] International newspapers were furious, but there was little that they could do – though journalists did try, whenever possible, to get information out of anyone involved.[37] Worldwide excitement increased even further when Harry Burton's photographs of the tomb and its treasures were first published in January 1923.[38] Carter found all of this attention frustrating; the flood of visitors and journalists got in the way of his work. To put this in context: a few years later, when Carter was still clearing and recording the treasures, the tomb received 12,300 visitors in just three months.[39] In 1914, the entire population of Luxor was 13,908.[40]

In the years that followed, the spread of Tut-mania made it impossible not to be influenced by ancient Egypt. There had been Egyptomania in the eighteenth and nineteenth centuries, but Tut-mania was of a greater magnitude. There were Tutankhamun-themed songs, such as 'Old King Tut',[41] and books, like the novel *The Kiss of Pharaoh: The Love Story of Tut-Anch-Amen*,[42] both released in 1923. Starring Boris Karloff, *The Mummy* was released in 1932. There were Tutankhamun and Egyptian-themed perfumes,[43] and in the United Kingdom, you could buy Tutankhamun pillows, sandals, clothing and even lemons.[44] The American magician Carter the Great – full name Charles Joseph Carter – felt the zeitgeist and used his surname to build his 1923 show around Tutankhamun.[45] Replicas of artefacts from Tutankhamun's antechamber, crafted over an eight-month period, featured in the British

Empire Exhibition at Wembley in 1924 and 1925 (where it was actually part of the associated amusement park), and then at Glasgow in 1938. Seeing this as a breach of copyright, Carter tried to have the exhibition shut down, but failed.[46] The media technology of the day, particularly photographs and films, helped Tutankhamun's name and the associated Egyptomania to spread. People saw Tutankhamun's belongings, objects similar to those that they used each day, and made connections to their own lives.[47]

34. A music sheet for the song 'In the Days of Tut-Ankh-Amen', performed in London in 1923.

THE DEATH OF LORD CARNARVON

As the months passed, Carter and Carnarvon came under extreme stress from various directions. In addition to the weight of carefully clearing the tomb and conserving its treasures for posterity, there was the ongoing and intense media interest, a relentless flow of tomb visitors, and arguments with the Egyptian government over the treasures' future – particularly whether Carnarvon should receive a share of them, something opposed by the authorities, or at least be paid for his years of funding the excavation. By the middle of February 1923, a furious argument erupted between the archaeologist and his wealthy sponsor; the exact cause isn't known, but given the stresses both were under, anything could have been the spark.[48] Afterwards, Carnarvon tried to mend the fracturing relationship, but a visit to Carter's house in early March ended with him being told to leave. If Carter had known what would happen next, he might have been more amiable.[49]

On 21 March 1923, Carter was in Cairo to see Carnarvon and noted in his diary that his benefactor was suffering from blood poisoning and erysipelas[50] – a bacterial infection. Fifteen days earlier, while shaving at the Winter Palace Hotel, Carnarvon had caught a mosquito bite with his razor. A fly had landed on the wound, and it became infected.[51] He soon developed a fever, but after some rest, appeared to be recovering. When Carter visited Carnarvon, still in Luxor, the two put their quarrel behind them, but all of a sudden the sickness returned. Carnarvon was moved to his suite at the Continental Hotel in Cairo, where Lady Carnarvon joined him on 26 March. Four days later, *The Times* reported that he was suffering from pneumonia.

Lord Carnarvon died at the Continental Hotel at 2 a.m. on 5 April 1923, his wife, daughter and son at his side.[52]

While obituaries appeared in the world press, for Carter, work had to continue – there was only a limited amount of time each season, and before long he would have to return to England. Once Carnarvon's body had left Cairo, Carter departed for Luxor, already assured by Lady Carnarvon that his right to work in the Valley of the Kings would continue under her name.[53]

THE MUMMY'S CURSE

Carnarvon's death led to widespread talk of a mummy's curse.[54] Arthur Conan Doyle, author of the Sherlock Holmes books, believed that 'elementals' were responsible for killing Carnarvon. Tales spread that Carnarvon's dog had died at Highclere Castle moments after his owner; while at the very same time, all of Cairo was plunged into darkness. A mark or scab, found on Tutankhamun's face, apparently mirrored the location of the mosquito bite on Carnarvon's face. And any misfortune experienced by those who entered Tutankhamun's tomb (plus their family and friends) was linked to the curse, no matter how long after the event the misfortune occurred. It was also said that an inscription promised death to those who disturbed the tomb, and that Carter's pet canary was eaten by a snake when the team first explored its chambers[55] – the curse's first undeserving victim. Carter was so irritated by these claims of curses and supernatural dangers that in the second volume of his publications on Tutankhamun's tomb, he took trouble to emphasize how ridiculous they were and that the tomb was perfectly safe.[56]

One of the reasons that so many curse stories appeared was the exclusive deal between *The Times* and Carnarvon: Tutankhamun sold newspapers, but the information that journalists received was second-hand. To make a splash, they had to find other ways to get Tutankhamun on their pages. There was nothing barring them from covering Carnarvon's death, and speculation of a supernatural connection was fed by the popular association between Egyptian tombs and dangerous forces. The trope of Egyptian curses had existed for some time before the discovery of Tutankhamun's tomb, and even featured in H. Rider Haggard's 1889 novel *Cleopatra*, in which the queen dies because she stole treasures.[57] Curses, supernatural powers and deaths made good news stories. Yet if there was a curse, it was a sluggish one. Carter lived until 1939. Lady Evelyn died aged seventy-eight in 1980. Douglas Derry, who unwrapped the king and performed the autopsy, lived to turn eighty-seven in 1961.[58]

MOVING AND DISPLAYING THE TREASURES

While Carnarvon's funeral was being held in England on 28 April, Carter wrote to Pierre Lacau, now head of Egypt's antiquities service, to discuss the transportation of Tutankhamun's treasures from the Valley of the Kings. A week later, he started packing the artefacts cleared from the tomb that season, a process that lasted for several days. In the end, he had eighty-nine boxes ready for shipment to Cairo – first though, they had to reach the Nile.[59] This heavy, sweaty and time-consuming work had to be done by hand. Egyptians loaded the boxes onto rail carts that rode on short spans of temporary track in the Valley of the Kings, and carefully pushed them down the Theban hills towards the Nile. But there was only a limited amount of track, so each time it ran out, men had to disassemble the used track and lay it on the ground ahead.[60]

35. Egyptians transporting Tutankhamun's treasures from the Valley of the Kings in crates, pushed on carts along tracks.

36. Egyptians carrying Tutankhamun's treasures in crates to a boat on the Nile. The treasures were taken to Cairo and unpacked at the Egyptian Museum.

Once the artefacts were safely sailing along the Nile to Cairo under the protection of antiquities guards and police, Carter made his own way to the city to meet Lacau, who was preparing to exhibit the treasures in the Egyptian Museum. After helping to unpack the most interesting artefacts for display and placing them in their cases, Carter left for England, putting an end to his dramatic season of excavation and research. From relative obscurity to the pages of every newspaper on earth, over the course of several months, Carter and Tutankhamun had gained international fame. That summer, Carter was even invited to a garden party at Buckingham Palace.[61] But his success was tinged with sadness and increasing pressure. The archaeologist had lost his friend and sponsor, there was the infuriating talk of a curse, and the world's curious and critical gaze was now squarely on everything he did. People were hungry for information, for him to work faster, to see results.[62] And the work ahead remained an immense challenge.

TROUBLE WITH THE GOVERNMENT

When Carter returned to work in Tutankhamun's tomb in November 1923, his main aim was to reach the king's sarcophagus, and this meant dismantling the gilded wooden shrines that surrounded it. This process alone took around four months and involved a lot of careful manoeuvring in the tight space of the burial chamber. When the sarcophagus was finally revealed, dignitaries once again gathered in the tomb to witness an historic event. As they watched, Carter's team lifted the sarcophagus lid using a series of pulleys, raising it with a rope above its basin. Slowly, light crept into the sarcophagus for the first time in over three thousand years. The king's outermost gilded coffin inched into view, obscured beneath a shroud.[63] Another barrier had been removed; soon, Carter must have thought, he would come face to face with Tutankhamun himself.

But the next day, long-simmering tensions between Carter and the Egyptian government boiled over into open dispute when Lacau forbade him from showing the wives of his team members the gilded coffin lying in the sarcophagus. To the authorities, Carter's invitation went against their official visitation instructions – instructions to which the archaeologist had earlier agreed. But to Carter, the Egyptian government had been increasingly interfering in his work and this was the latest insult. Just the day before, when he'd opened Tutankhamun's sarcophagus, the Minister of Public Works had changed the agreed schedule at the last minute – and worse, Carter had found the tone of the letter offensive. In defiance, he went to the Winter Palace Hotel and pinned a letter to a notice board, declaring that he and his team would stop work. Tutankhamun's sarcophagus lid was left dangling from a rope above its basin. The government retaliated immediately. They took control of the tomb and locked Carter out.[64]

In 1922, the British government had loosened its grip over Egypt, giving the country a form of independence. Although the United Kingdom continued to manage Egypt's foreign affairs (and kept control of the Suez Canal), they allowed elections, giving Egyptians the freedom to choose their own parliament and manage their own affairs, at least at home.[65] Carter's anger at being told who was allowed to visit the tomb and the response from Egypt's authorities reflected the reality that Tutankhamun's tomb did not belong to him[66] – a reality that he appears not yet to have accepted.

But there were other tensions too.

The Egyptian authorities were angry that *The Times* continued to receive the first updates on news from the tomb; and there was the ongoing matter of whether Lord Carnarvon's estate should receive a share of the treasures in return for funding the excavation. This latter problem, at least, was resolved when Lady Carnarvon agreed that the treasures should be kept in Egypt. In return, Egypt later gave the Carnarvon estate £36,000 to cover the cost of the excavation. The situation was improving, but it would still take almost a year for Carter and the Egyptian government to reach an agreement, enabling him to continue work in the tomb. During this time, Carter gave lectures about Tutankhamun in the United States and Canada.[67]

37. Tutankhamun's gold mask, still in position on his mummy.

UNWRAPPING TUTANKHAMUN

Carter arrived back in Egypt for his next excavation season on 28 September 1925,[68] and quickly set to work opening Tutankhamun's coffins. Having removed the pins that held the lid to the base of the outermost coffin, the team used a scaffold with a pulley system to lift it open. A second coffin lay within, and when this was opened, there was a third, made from solid gold. The ancient embalmers had poured so much liquid resin over the innermost coffin that it was glued to the inside of the second. Unable to separate them, the team carried the coffins – one still inside the other – into the antechamber, where they lifted the innermost coffin's lid to reveal Tutankhamun's mummy. His gold mask stared at the ceiling beneath a linen veil. Carter began to remove the items from the mummy, and found that the liquids poured over it had caused the outer wrappings to decay. When he tried to lift the mummy from the coffin, it was stuck firm to the base.

On 1 November, Tutankhamun left his tomb for the first time in thousands of years. Ten men carried the two coffins that contained his mummy up the tomb's entrance corridor and across the Valley of the Kings towards their laboratory in the tomb of King Seti II. But rather than take him inside, they placed the coffins down in the blazing sun, hoping that its heat would weaken and melt the hardened resin that sealed the mummy and coffins together. It didn't work. They tried again the next day. Nothing. With this second failure, they gave up on the plan and decided to unwrap Tutankhamun anyway. The event was set for 11 November and would take place in the tomb of Seti II.[69]

Watched by various dignitaries, and assisted by Saleh Bey Hamdi,[70] the anatomist Douglas Derry coated Tutankhamun's wrappings in a thin layer of melted paraffin wax.[71] When this cooled, he was able to make an incision through the disintegrating bandages, undoing the work of the ancient embalmers. His knife passed straight down the centre. He opened the stiffened bandages like a set of double doors.[72] The group peered deeper within the mummy bundle, but to their disappointment, the wrappings were, on the whole, deteriorated. Meanwhile, the solidified resin continued to hold Tutankhamun's body to his coffin, as if unwilling to let the boy king go. Moving through the layers of wrappings, the team removed amulet after amulet – symbols of protection made of gold and precious stones, failing in their intended function.[73] This process continued over the following days, until Derry and Hamdi reached the final wrappings covering the king's corpse. First, they revealed his knees and feet. The legs were brittle, Derry noticed, and he could lift the skin right off the bone. Then, they moved up to the torso.[74]

Tutankhamun's body was in a terrible state of preservation.

Along with the amulets, the team found the king's jewellery and accoutrements – rings, sandals and daggers.[75] But to remove them, they first had to dismember Tutankhamun's corpse. They separated the teenage king's limbs – the arms coming away at the elbows and the hands freed at the wrists – and cut across his torso just above the hips, slicing his upper body away from its lower half. Now able to reach beneath the torso, they freed it from the coffin's hardened resin.[76] In the end, only the king's head remained, held firm by resin within his gold mask, itself stuck to the inside of the coffin. Carter and his team used heated knives to melt the resin,[77] releasing the king's decapitated head, but leaving his mask glued to the coffin. They unwrapped the layers of linen from around the head, finding more and more treasures, until just a single, fragile layer of linen remained. It disintegrated, bringing the boy king's face into the light once more.[78]

Tutankhamun stared back at the doctors and archaeologists.

Howard Carter had reached his goal, but to get there, he had torn apart the object of his dreams.

7

A Century of Tut-Mania

Tutankhamun's autopsy was over. Freed from his wrappings, amulets and jewels, the king remained in the unfamiliar surroundings of the tomb of King Seti II – the laboratory – until the next excavation season. In the meantime, Carter melted the resin that held the two royal coffins together, and when its grip loosened, pulled the gold mask free. The heat also freed the mask's glass and stone inlays. Some fell off, leaving Carter to spend precious time fixing them back in place.[1] He then packed the innermost coffin and gold mask for their journey from the Valley of the Kings to Luxor's train station on the Nile's east bank. Their next stop was Cairo,[2] where the mask would amaze visitors to the Egyptian Museum from January 1926.[3]

Eventually, Carter reconstructed Tutankhamun's dismembered mummy on a tray on a bed of sand, imitating the body's original, complete, appearance. It now looked as if it had never been touched.[4] He then returned the king to his outermost coffin – the body still lying in the sand tray – which in turn was lowered into the sarcophagus in his tomb. The team sealed the coffin, hiding Tutankhamun from view, but left the sarcophagus open. It was covered with a sheet of glass so that curious visitors could peer within.[5] This took place on 23 October 1926; over the following years, Carter cleared the treasury and then the annexe, and by the end of November 1930, the tomb was empty.[6] The final conservation work ended in 1932, bringing the grand project to an end, a decade after it had begun.

Now that the majority of Tutankhamun's treasures had been moved to Cairo, visitors from across the world could see a select number of them in the Egyptian Museum, experiencing their own sense of wonder and discovery. Meanwhile, diagnosed with Hodgkin's disease soon after completing his work in the tomb, Carter spent his final years dividing his time between London and Luxor. He died on 2 March 1939, and was buried in Putney Vale Cemetery, London.[7] This marked the end of an important phase in the boy king's afterlife, but the story of Tutankhamun would continue without his discoverer. Six months after Carter's death, the Second World War broke out, and the Egyptian Museum's curators took many of Tutankhamun's treasures to the basement of the building for safekeeping.[8] Tutankhamun's mummy, still resting in his tomb in the Valley of the Kings, was less lucky – and it would be decades before anyone realized his fate.

AUDIENCES WITH THE PHARAOH

On 4 December 1968, a team of researchers, led by Ronald Harrison of the University of Liverpool and accompanied by a TV crew, entered Tutankhamun's burial chamber to x-ray the mummy. They would be the first to study the body since Douglas Derry's autopsy in the 1920s. The team removed the glass that sealed Tutankhamun's sarcophagus and opened the coffin, believing that it hadn't been touched since Carter placed the king inside. They were wrong. When the team revealed Tutankhamun's body, not only did everyone discover that it had been dismembered – something absent from the official publications – but even more surprising, they saw that it no longer rested in the position that Carter had left it. Tutankhamun's arms lay at his sides, rather than crossed over his belly. His penis had fallen into the coffin. His ears and eyes were damaged. Some of the king's bones were placed beside his head. The linen that covered the body had gone missing. And on top of all this, Tutankhamun's beaded skullcap and the beaded collar that covered his chest, both left in place by Carter, had vanished.

What had happened? The only explanation is that at some point in the intervening decades, looters disturbed the body. This probably happened during the Second World War, when security was weak in the Valley of the Kings. Without mentioning these revelations, while the cameras rolled, the researchers took their x-rays, scanning each piece of the disarticulated mummy, one by one, and spent a few hours putting Tutankhamun's body back into order – all except for a skin sample, which was taken to the United Kingdom. Then, they resealed the boy king in his coffin.[9] It was not for the last time.

Since the 1960s, Tutankhamun has been awoken from his eternal sleep four times. The first was in 1978, when orthodontist James E. Harris opened the coffin to x-ray the pharaoh's head.[10] The second, a few decades later, was more dramatic. In 2004, Egypt's antiquities department under its secretary general, Zahi Hawass, initiated a project to CT-scan the pharaohs. This technology would digitally slice through their fragile bodies, providing new details about their lives and deaths, but, importantly, would do no damage to them. Driven in a trailer, the CT-scanning machine was taken to the Valley of the Kings, where, on the evening of 5 January 2005, following a storm, Tutankhamun was raised, once again, from his coffin and sarcophagus. He then went on a short journey. For the first time since the 1920s, he was carried from his burial chamber, through the antechamber, and out of his tomb into the night.

The trailer was parked just outside the tomb. It took only half an hour for his body to be recorded in the scanning machine, transforming his remains into data, preserving him in a way that would have made his embalmers envious. Afterwards, the king returned to rest in his coffin.[11]

Tutankhamun was next moved on 5 November 2007, when the antiquities service transferred his mummy from the burial chamber to a transparent, climate controlled case in a corner of the antechamber.[12] This better ensured his body's preservation for the future, and, for the first time, gave visitors the chance to look down into the face of Egypt's most famous pharaoh. Since then, there has been only one further interaction with his body, on 24 February 2008, when researchers, led by Zahi Hawass, took DNA samples as part of a wider project to study Egypt's royal family connections.[13]

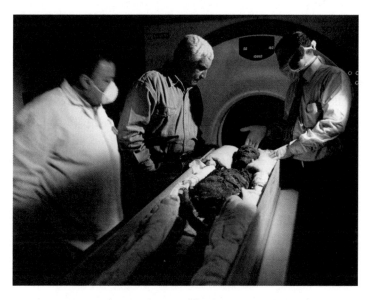

38. Egypt's former Minister of Antiquities Zahi Hawass performs a CT-scan on the mummy of Tutankhamun.

As of writing, Tutankhamun remains in his tomb, staring up at the antechamber's bare ceiling. The only pharaoh we know of still resting in his own tomb.

INVESTIGATING TUTANKHAMUN'S HEALTH AND DEATH

What did the results of these various post-mortem audiences with the boy king tell us? Over the years, researchers have looked at the same evidence and diagnosed Tutankhamun with a vast range of illnesses and physical problems. He may have had coeliac disease, Wilson's disease, Klippel-Feil syndrome, a metabolic disorder, Froehlich's syndrome, epilepsy, plague, tuberculosis, bilharzia, sickle-cell disease, Gaucher disease or tumours. His occipital bones are too thick, or conversely, too thin. Hopefully, he didn't have all of these problems at once. The recent DNA study showed that he suffered from a particularly powerful form of malaria, while the CT-scans indicated oligodactyly, Köhler disease II, and Freiberg-Köhler syndrome, and that he lived with a clubfoot, leaving him with difficulty walking. The large number of sticks found in Tutankhamun's tomb, and ancient images of him leaning on a staff and hunting while sitting, have been cited to support this argument.[14]

Nonetheless, a recent examination of Tutankhamun's sticks and staves found only slight signs of wear on their tips, the opposite of what we would expect if he relied on them to move around. Perhaps, he simply used them as symbols of power and status,[15] or perhaps his servants carried him around in a palanquin. It's also possible that the problems identified in Tutankhamun's legs and feet were caused by the treatment of his mummy.[16] Ronald Harrison's notes on Tutankhamun's feet, made during his x-ray study in the 1960s, do not report any unusual features. But he does mention that he'd been told of an occasion when Carter's team, wanting to melt and study some of the resin on the body, put a blow lamp against one of the feet. This perhaps explains why the toes of the left foot are basically skeletal and lack any resin coating.[17]

Exactly how Tutankhamun died still remains a mystery, but many explanations have been put forward over the past century. Perhaps the best-known suggestion is that he was murdered, based on a dislodged piece of the boy king's skull found lying within his skull cavity. This argument captured the popular imagination, but more recent investigations showed that the piece of skull most likely fell after his death. Other causes of death offered over the years include a hippo attack, an insect bite, that the king died in a chariot accident, or that he was kicked in the chest by a horse.[18] The CT-scans and DNA studies, meanwhile, suggest that a number of factors might have contributed to Tutankhamun's death. According to Zahi Hawass and his research team, the combination of malaria, clubfoot and bone problems might have left the king quite weak. And when he severely broke his leg near the time of his death – perhaps just a few days before – he may have developed septicaemia. If Tutankhamun had been in an accident, perhaps even just a fall, and injured himself, he may have been simply too weak to recover.[19]

After studying these same CT-scans, Ben Harer argued that Tutankhamun's heart, sternum and pieces of his ribs were already missing when he was mummified, showing that the king had experienced an injury that severely wounded his upper torso. He adds that Tutankhamun's diaphragm remains whole because there was no need for the embalmers to break it to reach the lungs (as normally happened), and that they sawed off the ends of his ribs.[20] But Salima Ikram has argued that the ribs could have been sawn off in more recent times, when the other damage to the mummy may have happened, while the heart could have been deliberately removed by the ancient embalmers or lost at the same time as the king's beaded collar.[21] Despite all of the research and technological advancements, then, many interpretations remain.

How and why Tutankhamun truly died may forever remain a mystery.

TOURING EXHIBITIONS AND A NEW WAVE OF TUT-MANIA

After decades on display in the Egyptian Museum, Cairo, Tutankhamun's treasures left Egypt for the first time in November 1961, when they were exhibited at the National Gallery of Art in Washington, DC. The aim was to raise awareness about the looming loss of archaeological sites in Nubia, which would be submerged by the lake created by the construction of the Aswan High Dam. Egypt and UNESCO needed funding for a project to rescue some of these monuments, and though the exhibition didn't directly raise this money, lectures helped to show the scale of the task ahead and made it easier for people to understand the need for public funding. Over the following years, the artefacts travelled across the United States, and then on to Canada and Japan.[22] In 1967, they were displayed at the Petit Palais in Paris, where the exhibition included a crowd-pleasing star absent from the earlier tour: Tutankhamun's gold mask. At this point, the exhibitions started directly raising funds for the Nubian monuments campaign. Temples were in danger, and Tutankhamun's influence brought about their protection – it was a situation that the king would have recognized well. The exhibition next travelled to the

British Museum, London, in 1972 and across the USSR from 1973 to 1975.

Tutankhamun's treasures made their next international journey from 1976 to 1979, when they again travelled across the United States and to Canada. Museums capitalized on the boy king's fame by selling Tutankhamun-themed clothing, bags, jewellery, books, children's games and expensive replicas.[23] Across the cities visited, shops sold Tut-themed goods, from wallpaper to furniture; if you'd ever wanted to own a Tutankhamun sleeping bag, that was the time to get it.[24] People queued for hours to buy tickets, and each museum welcomed hundreds of thousands of visitors. Many of them must have bought Steve Martin's 1978 song 'King Tut', because it sold over a million copies.[25] From 1980 to 1981, the exhibition toured West Germany, before returning home. The treasures didn't leave Egypt again for a couple of decades. Starting in 2004, the more recent tours travelled the world in different forms until 2020, when the onset of the Covid-19 pandemic led Egypt's authorities to bring them back to Cairo, with a brief stop for twenty artefacts at museums in Sharm el-Sheikh and Hurghada.[26] Tutankhamun's gold mask was absent from these exhibitions – it is never expected to leave Egypt again.

REPLICA EXHIBITIONS

One of the dangers facing any exhibition tour, and indeed, any artefact on display, is the possibility of damage. Ancient artefacts are fragile and need constant care. Any handling, even for cleaning, can be a critical time. One wrong move and an object that has survived for thousands of years can be gone in an instant. Over the past century, Tutankhamun's treasures have not been immune from such dangers. The scorpion atop the head of a figurine of the goddess Selket was damaged during its installation for the 1980 Berlin Tutankhamun exhibition, causing anger in Egypt.[27] And the beard on Tutankhamun's gold mask came loose in 2014 when museum staff were fixing the lighting in its case. They reattached it badly with epoxy glue, leaving marks on the golden face. When this came to light in 2015, the museum authorities had to carefully remove the beard and glue, and find a better method to re-attach it, a process that took two months.[28]

One way of giving people access to ancient artefacts, whilst keeping the originals safe, is to create accurate replicas. The first replicas of Tutankhamun's treasures were made for the British Empire Exhibition of 1924. Subsequently bought by Albert Reckitt of Hull, in the late 1930s they were displayed in the city's Mortimer Museum and then in a local warehouse transformed into a gallery. In 1972 they were on show once more, to coincide with the British Museum's Tutankhamun exhibition. Today, these early replicas can be seen in Hull's Hands on History Museum.[29] More recently, Semmel Exhibitions created a touring exhibition of replica Tutankhamun artefacts, displaying them both as individual objects and in recreations of the tomb chambers at the moment of discovery. By January 2019, this exhibition had been visited by more than 6.5 million people at venues across the globe.[30] Egypt's Ministry of Antiquities also produced its own replica exhibition, which has travelled as far afield as Rabat in Morocco and Liège in Belgium.[31] Other replica artefacts can be seen in Dorchester in the United Kingdom,[32] and Las Vegas in the United States,[33] among many other places around the world.

Protecting Tutankhamun's tomb – itself a huge tourist draw – has also been a major concern over the past century. Humidity, dust build-up (and consequently the need for dusting, which can cause harm), and accidental scratches caused by tourists and film crews damaged the burial chamber's paintings as the decades passed. To clean and protect them, from 2009 to 2018, the Egyptian authorities worked with the Getty Conservation Institute. As well as conserving the paintings, such as by securing flaking paint, they carefully removed dust and installed a new ventilation system to prevent future build-up. The team also investigated brown spots of mould that covered the walls, already present when Carter opened the tomb. Luckily, they found that the microorganisms causing these spots were dead, and could not spread further.[34]

In recent years, Howard Carter's house at the foot of the Valley of the Kings – 'Castle Carter' – has itself become a tourist attraction. A hologram of the famous archaeologist welcomes guests, a digital afterlife that he could never have predicted for himself. But just as Carter has been replicated, so has Tutankhamun's burial chamber – right beside his old

39. Howard Carter's house at the foot of the Valley of the Kings was known as 'Castle Carter'.

house. Opened on 30 April 2014, this life-size facsimile was the creation of Factum Arte, who laser scanned the tomb's walls in extreme 3D detail over the course of three months in 2009.[35] The scanning quality was so high that not only were the paintings recorded, but also every crack and bump in the walls' surfaces. The team also reproduced the king's sarcophagus, while the exhibition attached to the facsimile includes a section of the painted decoration that was dismantled when Carter removed the wall leading from the burial chamber into the antechamber.[36] The results of these scans were placed online for anyone to explore, and played an important role in one of the most recent media frenzies surrounding Tutankhamun.

SECRET CHAMBERS IN TUTANKHAMUN'S TOMB?

In 2015, Tutankhamun made the news once again when Nicholas Reeves published a paper arguing that hidden chambers could lie behind the walls of the boy king's tomb. Using Factum Arte's 3D laser scan results,[37] Reeves looked at the texture of the walls – removing the painted decoration – and noticed anomalies, which he theorized could be sealed doorways to further chambers. One might lead to an extra storeroom, he wrote, while the other could be the entrance to the burial of Queen Nefertiti.[38] Building his evidence, he argued that the paintings on one of the walls appeared to have originally been made for Nefertiti, while the wall niches for the king's magic bricks were carved in places where they couldn't break through into the hidden chambers.[39] Reeves' theory met with huge media interest, and Egypt's antiquities department invited experts to perform geophysical scans in the tomb, enabling them to see what might lie behind its walls. If secret chambers existed, they'd find them.

The results of the first set of scans, taken in November 2015, suggested that metallic and organic items were hidden behind the tomb's walls, along with empty spaces.[40] Excitement grew. But a second set, taken in 2016, contradicted these conclusions, finding no evidence of secret chambers.[41] A third investigation in 2018 also found nothing.[42] With three scans conducted, and two finding only solid rock, it appeared unlikely that any hidden chambers existed. The media moved on, but Reeves continued to develop his theory. He focused his analysis on the tomb's decoration, and asked an independent expert to study the geophysical scan results.[43] Later, he published animations explaining his theories.[44] Intriguingly, in addition to Reeves' work, further anomalies have been identified in the vicinity of Tutankhamun's tomb, though they are not directly connected to it. Whether these are natural voids in the rock or the result of human action can only be confirmed by excavation.[45]

THE GRAND EGYPTIAN MUSEUM

Having spent most of the past century in the Egyptian Museum, Cairo, or travelling the world, Tutankhamun's treasures have now made their new home at the Grand Egyptian Museum in Giza. This museum, planned and under construction since the early 2000s, was built around 2 kilometres from the pyramids of Giza, west of central Cairo, in a location now equipped with its own airport (the Sphinx International Airport). Only around one third of Tutankhamun's treasures were previously on display in Cairo, but in their new home, visitors will be able to see all of them. This amounts to around 5,000 artefacts,[46] including his famous gold mask (which, incidentally, was recreated using coffee cups at the Grand Egyptian Museum in December 2019, forming a Guinness world record-breaking coffee cup mosaic[47]). In total, the museum will house around 100,000 artefacts illustrating ancient Egyptian history, and has enough space – 60,000 square metres – to display half of them.

To bring all of the royal treasures together, Tutankhamun's artefacts at Luxor Museum were transferred to Giza in 2018,[48] joined in 2019 by his outermost coffin, previously exhibited in his tomb in the Valley of the Kings. For most of the past century, the king rested in this coffin, but with his mummy now in a climate-controlled case, and cracks starting to impact the coffin's structure, the time came for it to leave the tomb.[49] In preparation for their new display, Tutankhamun's treasures have been studied and conserved in the Grand Egyptian Museum's conservation lab. The king's tunics were among them, giving researchers an insight into how they were made and the dyes used to create their colours.[50] His sun canopy has been studied with a digital microscope, as have his chariots.[51]

40. Conserving Tutankhamun's lion-headed ritual couch at the Grand Egyptian Museum, Giza.

This research confirmed that the canopy was once part of a royal chariot, providing Tutankhamun and Ankhesenamun with shade while they rode at ceremonial events.[52] Even previously unnoticed artefacts, such as clay seals, kept in boxes since Carter's time, have come to light.[53] Through such work, the story of Tutankhamun is constantly evolving.

THE NEXT CENTURY

Tutankhamun is now entering his next century reborn in the land of the living, one hundred years after his tomb's discovery. Although it is his treasures that catch the eyes – the gold mask, gilded coffins and colourful jewellery – these are only one part of his story. Another part is found in his walking sticks and sandals, tunics and wine jars, toys and heirlooms. It is through these artefacts that we meet the teenager behind the mask and jewels. Every detail prised from them is a piece of a historical jigsaw slotted into place. They tell the story of a young man, whose life ended early. He had a wife, tried to have children, and grew up in troubled times – much like many people today. Investigations into his body show the health problems that he lived with, in a period when there was little doctors could do to ease a patient's suffering. As the next century passes and scientific methods of analysis become increasingly advanced, his mummy will undoubtedly be raised from its rest many times. These will solve existing mysteries – and create new ones.

Tutankhamun's virtually intact tomb was not just a place of burial, but a time capsule reflecting a much wider world. This is another part of the story. When you stare at his treasures, remember the miners that toiled in Egypt's Eastern Desert and Nubia to bring the gold to the royal workshops. Think of traders sailing on the Mediterranean Sea, or walking with donkeys, bearing bags of precious stones and metals. Remember those who stitched the king's clothing and hammered the gold, who carved the wood, and painted the statuettes. These are the forgotten multitudes behind the treasures, who live on through Tutankhamun's fame. Future investigations of the artefacts will reveal more about their lives, resurrecting their role in the creation of the treasure. The story of Tutankhamun is theirs too.

There's also more to learn about Tutankhamun's family. Debate continues around who his father truly was, and much of this hinges on the identity of the skeleton found in KV 55. New scientific techniques might help to solve this mystery in the coming decades. The lucky turn of a trowel may finally uncover an inscription bearing the name of Tutankhamun's mother, or reveal where King Neferneferuaten – the famous Nefertiti – was buried. Archaeologists might also discover the fate of Tutankhamun's half-sisters. Did he rebury those who died at Amarna in tombs at Thebes, just as he did for Queen Tiye and seemingly Akhenaten? What happened to his half-sisters who survived into his reign? And then there's Ankhesenamun. Over recent years, archaeologists have been scouring the Valley of the Kings for the queen's lost tomb.[54] If they are successful, perhaps it will be Tutankhamun's wife, rather than the famous boy king himself, who takes the limelight for the next century.

Endnotes

INTRODUCTION

1 The chronology followed in this book is adapted from that presented in Dodson, *Amarna Sunset*, 168–171.

2 The pit is KV 54 and the small chamber is KV 58; KV stands for King's Valley. Davis, *The Tombs of Harmhabi and Touatânkhamanou*, 2–3, where the date of the discovery of KV 58 is incorrectly given as 1907. Reeves and Wilkinson, *The Complete Valley of the Kings*, 126 (for KV 54) and 186 (for KV 58).

3 For those who want more than the story, who want to see the nuts and bolts and onward references, the endnotes provide information about the artefacts and other evidence on which the reconstruction is based. Throughout the endnotes, you'll see that I often refer to 'Carter numbers'. These are the numbers that Howard Carter assigned to each object during the clearance of Tutankhamun's tomb. To find out more about each artefact, look up the Carter number on the Griffith Institute's 'Tutankhamun: Anatomy of an Excavation' webpage, in the 'Object Cards' section. http://www.griffith.ox.ac.uk/discoveringTut/

I. THE STORY OF TUTANKHATEN

1 Dodson, *Amarna Sunset*, 13. For more details about Amarna, see Kemp, *The City of Akhenaten and Nefertiti*.

2 This event is based on scenes from the Tomb of Meryre II and the Tomb of Huya at Tell el-Amarna. See: Tomb of Meryre II in Davies, *The Rock Tombs of El Amarna*, vol. 2, 38–43; Tomb of Huya in Davies, *The Rock Tombs of El Amarna*, vol. 3, 9–12.

3 As suggested by Dodson, *Amarna Sunset*, 13.

4 Given that this was the main residence of the Amarna royals, it is probable that this is where Tutankhamun was born.

5   For birth bricks and the pavilions in which women gave birth, see Janssen and Janssen, *Growing Up and Getting Old in Ancient Egypt*, 4–7.

6   Hawass and Saleem, *Scanning the Pharaohs*, 97–100; Fagan, *Lord and Pharaoh*, 42.

7   Even with the addition of DNA studies, there remains debate over Tutankhamun's parents. Candidates for his mother include the famous Queen Nefertiti, Queen Kiya, or a currently unknown sister of Akhenaten. Her body has been found, however. See note 8 below.

8   The mummy known as the Younger Lady from KV 35 has been identified as Tutankhamun's mother, see Hawass et al., 'Ancestry and Pathology in King Tutankhamun's Family', 641; for the fractures in the mummy's skull and her age at death, see Hawass and Saleem, *Scanning the Pharaohs*, 80–83.

9   Maia is known from her tomb at Saqqara. See Zivie, *La Tombe de Maïa*.

10 Zivie, 'From Maïa to Meritaten', 47–60.

11 It was a practice known since the Old Kingdom and is described in myths of the gods. Roehrig, *The Eighteenth Dynasty Titles Royal Nurse...*, 314–315.

12 Roehrig, *The Eighteenth Dynasty Titles Royal Nurse...*, 267–268.

13 Aye's family connections are still debated. Here, I follow the argument that he is a son of Yuya and Tuya, who were also the parents of Tiye, who became wife of King Amenhotep III. See, for example, Van Dijk, 'Horemheb and the Struggle for the Throne of Tutankhamun', 32. I take the title God's Father, often used by Aye, to mean an individual with a close adviser role to the king; see Roehrig, *The Eighteenth Dynasty Titles Royal Nurse...*, 351–356.

14 As a result, she is one of the best attested women at Amarna outside the royal family. Roehrig, *The Eighteenth Dynasty Titles Royal Nurse...*, 262–267.

15 Zivie, 'From Maïa to Meritaten', 47–60.

16 Carter no. 620(13).

17 The Global Egyptian Museum, http://www.globalegyptian museum.org/record.aspx?id=15067. The bird has no Carter no. but is listed among the toys in Alfred Lucas' conservation journal: Griffith Institute, http://www.griffith.ox.ac.uk/discoveringTut/conservation/4lucasn6.html.

18 Carter no. 585aa. Carter, *The Tomb of Tut.Ankh.Amen*, vol. 3, 121–122.

19 Lazaridis, 'Education and Apprenticeship', https://escholarship.org/uc/item/1026h44g.

20 This is an assumption, however it would be unrealistic for Amun's name to be attacked everywhere in the country, but left untouched

in teaching material. It is also an assumption that he read and copied *The Tale of Sinuhe*, but as it was a popular story for many centuries, including in the period when Tutankhamun lived, it seems probable. Although the protagonist of the story is typically referred to as Sinuhe, his name is more correctly rendered as Sanehat. For a summary of the ancient sources for this tale, see: Digital Egypt for Universities, 'Tale of Sanehat: Two Principal Sources', https://www.ucl.ac.uk/museums-static/digitalegypt/literature/sanehat/sources.html.

21 Simpson et al., *The Literature of Ancient Egypt*, 152–165.

22 Simpson et al., *The Literature of Ancient Egypt*, 166–171.

23 Carter no. 271e(1). Reeves, *The Complete Tutankhamun*, 166.

24 Carter no. 147e. Reeves, *The Complete Tutankhamun*, 166.

25 From one box in Tutankhamun's tomb (Carter no. 271) came two small palettes, one bearing the name Tutankhaten (Carter no. 271e(2)) and the other Tutankhamun (Carter no. 271b). In these, the two ink pots, used to hold red and black ink, showed signs of use. Reeves, *The Complete Tutankhamun*, 166; Carter, *The Tomb of Tut.Ankh.Amen*, vol. 3, 80.

26 Carter no, 271f. See Reeves, *The Complete Tutankhamun*, 166.

27 When the palette (Carter no. 262) was discovered in Tutankhamun's tomb, the blue pigment was nearly empty. Allon and Navratilova, *Ancient Egyptian Scribes*, 67–76.

28 Due to confusion in understanding the tomb inscriptions, Sennedjem may actually have been called Senqed. See Kawai, *Studies in the Reign of Tutankhamun*, 439–446 for information on this individual.

29 Based on scenes in the tomb of Sennedjem at Akhmim. Kawai, *Studies in the Reign of Tutankhamun*, 445. This scene is sometimes interpreted as Tutankhamun riding with the future King Aye. Darnell and Manassa, *Tutankhamun's Armies*, 52.

30 Gloves worn while riding chariots were found in Tutankhamun's tomb, e.g. Carter no. 50u. Vogelsang-Eastwood, *Tutankhamun's Wardrobe*, 88–89; Fagan, *Lord and Pharaoh*, 45. For the gloves in general, see Reeves, *The Complete Tutankhamun*, 156–157.

31 Several socks were found in Tutankhamun's tomb. See Vogelsang-Eastwood, 'Socks', 165–168.

32 McLeod, *Composite Bows from the Tomb of Tutankhamun*, 23 and 30–31.

33 Carter no. 585z and 585cc; Carter, *The Tomb of Tut.Ankh.Amen*, vol. 3, 121.

34 Carter no. 585y; Carter, *The Tomb of Tut.Ankh.Amen*, vol. 3, 121–123.

35 Roehrig, *The Eighteenth Dynasty Titles Royal Nurse...*, 325–326.

36 Shaw, *The Pharaoh*, 54–61.

37 For an overview of Akhenaten's religious reforms, see Shaw, *Egyptian Mythology*, 124–129.

38 See, for example, Arnold, *The Royal Women of Amarna*, 17.

39 Tyldesley, *Nefertiti's Face*, 44–45.

40 Tyldesley, *Nefertiti's Face*, 30–31.

41 For the Workmen's Village, see Amarna Project, 'Workmen's Village', https://www.amarnaproject.com/pages/amarna_the_place/workmans_village/index.shtml.

42 Habicht, Eppenberger and Rühli, 'A Critical Assessment of Proposed Outbreaks of Plague and Other Epidemic Diseases in Ancient Egypt', 218. Fleas that carry the bubonic plague have been uncovered during excavations at the Workmen's Village at Amarna, see: Singer, 'Beyond Amarna', 237–238, and for the symptoms of bubonic plague, 229.

43 Amarna letter EA 35. See Singer, 'Beyond Amarna', 224–226.

44 Singer, 'Beyond Amarna', 226–229.

45 Dodson, *Amarna Sunset*, 18.

46 Dodson, *Amarna Sunset*, 18–23; Van Dijk, 'The Death of Meketaten', 83–88.

47 Or perhaps even earlier.

48 Dodson, *Amarna Sunset*, 25–26.

49 The evidence and debate around the identity, co-regency and role of Smenkhkare is ongoing. For a recent analysis, summarizing the evidence and arguments, see Dodson, *Amarna Sunset*, 29–42.

50 Dodson, *Amarna Sunset*, 40.

51 To ensure a clear narrative, I've opted to see Neferneferuaten as Nefertiti rather than Meritaten, as some Egyptologists have proposed. I've also chosen to present Neferneferuaten as ruling alone, rather than in a co-regency with Tutankhamun, which has also been argued. For an overview of the various arguments surrounding Neferneferuaten's original identity, and the possibility that she ruled as a co-regent with Akhenaten, see Van der Perre, 'The Year 16 Graffito of Akhenaten in Dayr Abū Ḥinnis', 77–108. For the possibility that Neferneferuaten ruled as co-regent with Tutankhamun, see Dodson, *Amarna Sunset*, 45–47.

52 In the third year of Neferneferuaten's reign, an individual wrote a graffito on the wall of the Tomb of Pairy at Thebes. The text mentions the king's mortuary temple. See Dodson, *Amarna Sunset*, 43–45. In the New Kingdom, according to tradition, the king had a burial in the Valley of the Kings, and a mortuary temple in the plains below.

53 See, for example, Eaton-Krauss, *The Unknown Tutankhamun*, 106–107.

54 Assuming that Tutankhamun's sarcophagus originally belonged to Neferneferuaten. See Eaton-Krauss, *The Unknown Tutankhamun*, 88–92.

55 These were reused in Tutankhamun's burial. The gold bands are Carter no. 256b 1–4; the small gold coffins are Carter no. 266g 1–4; and the pectoral is Carter no. 261p(1). See Eaton-Krauss, *The Unknown Tutankhamun*, 106–107.

56 Here, I'm following the argument that Tutankhamun's famous gold mask (Carter no. 256a) was originally made for Neferneferuaten, but that the face was replaced when it was used by Tutankhamun. For this argument and the evidence that supports it, see Reeves, 'Tutankhamun's Mask Reconsidered'; and Reeves, 'The Gold Mask of Ankhkheperure Neferneferuaten', 77–79. For a summary, see Eaton-Krauss, *The Unknown Tutankhamun*, 111.

57 Ogden, 'Metals', 161–162; Klemm and Klemm, *Gold and Gold Mining in Ancient Egypt and Nubia*, 8–11.

58 Reeves, 'Tutankhamun's Mask Reconsidered', 513, note 18.

59 Reeves, 'Tutankhamun's Mask Reconsidered', 515–516.

60 Uda, Ishizaki and Baba, 'Tutankhamun's Gold Mask and Throne', 153.

61 For lapis lazuli, see Moorey, *Ancient Mesopotamian Materials and Industries*, 85–92; for the trade route to Egypt see 85 and 90; for accessibility to the mines and extracting the stone, 87; and for its transportation as lumps, see 88.

62 Uda, Ishizaki and Baba, 'Tutankhamun's Gold Mask and Throne', 154. For the source of Egypt's amazonite, see Aston, Harrell and Shaw, 'Stone', 46, and for the sources of carnelian, 27.

63 Uda, Ishizaki and Baba, 'Tutankhamun's Gold Mask and Throne', 153.

64 Aston, Harrell and Shaw, 'Stone', 46–47.

65 Uda, Ishizaki and Baba, 'Tutankhamun's Gold Mask and Throne', 154–155.

66 Kawai, *Studies in the Reign of Tutankhamun*, 93.

67 Dodson, *Amarna Sunset*, 43.

68 Dodson, *Amarna Sunset*, 43. For the excavation of the house, see Amarna Project, 'House of Ranefer: Background', https://www.amarnaproject.com/pages/recent_projects/excavation/house_of_ranefer/.

2. RESTORING ORDER

1 The crook is Carter no. 44u. The flail is Carter no. 269f.
2 Carter no. 256:40.
3 Carter no. 256ppp.

4   On royal audiences, the decoration of throne rooms and the daily morning meeting with the vizier and other members of the court, see Shaw, *The Pharaoh*, 78–85.

5   My general summary of the coronation ceremony is based on Shaw, *The Pharaoh*, 64–69, with additional detail, specifically from Tutankhamun's reign, taken from a coronation stele from the reign of Tutankhamun published by Kawai, 'A Coronation Stela of Tutankhamun? (JdE 27076)', 637–644; and scenes from Luxor Temple, see: Kawai, *Studies in the Reign of Tutankhamun*, 221; Johnson, 'Honorific Figures of Amenhotep III in the Luxor Temple Colonnade Hall', 140; and Epigraphic Survey, *Reliefs and Inscriptions at Luxor Temple*, vol. 2, 21–22, and pl. 169.

6   On the king's divinity, see Shaw, *The Pharaoh*, 22–23.

7   Carter no. 21d. Larson, 'The Heb-sed Robe and the "Ceremonial Robe" of Tut'ankhamun', 180–181; Vogelsang-Eastwood, *Tutankhamun's Wardrobe*, 30 and 54.

8   Kawai, *Studies in the Reign of Tutankhamun*, 259. For Tutankhamun's coronation statues, see Metropolitan Museum of Art MMA 50.6 and Walters Art Museum 22.222.

9   Carter no. 54k. See Aldred, 'The "New Year Gifts" to the Pharaoh', 75–76. Vogelsang-Eastwood, *Tutankhamun's Wardrobe*, 100–101.

10 For the arguments regarding when Ankhesenamun was born, see Kawai, *Studies in the Reign of Tutankhamun*, 33–34 and 42.

11 Hawass, *Discovering Tutankhamun*, 35.

12 Ahmose is usually referred to as Ahmose I, but recent research has shown that there was an earlier King Ahmose, making him more correctly Ahmose II. See Biston-Moulin, 'Le roi Sénakht-en-Rê Ahmès de la XVIIe dynastie'.

13 Roth, 'Queen', 7.

14 In general, see Roth, 'Queen', 7. Ankhesenamun wrote letters to the Hittite king after Tutankhamun's death. See Chapter 5.

15 Robins, *Women in Ancient Egypt*, 42.

16 Two sistra, bearing signs of use, were found in Tutankhamun's tomb. These are Carter nos 75 and 76. Sistra were usually used only by women, but the person who gave these objects to the king's burial is not known. See Manniche, *Musical Instruments from the Tomb of Tutankhamun*, 5–6.

17 As shown in art. Roth, 'Queen', 6.

18 See the scenes on the Little Golden Shrine from Tutankhamun's tomb, Carter no. 108. For crowns, see Roth, 'Queen', 3.

19 The vulture headdress is often seen in images of queens. Roth, 'Queen', 2–3.

20 The foetuses were found in Tutankhamun's tomb and assigned Carter nos 317a and 317b. See Hawass and Saleem, *Scanning the Pharaohs*, 107–116.

21 This text survives on the Restoration Stele, originally erected at the Temple of Amun at Karnak, in modern Luxor. It is now in the Egyptian Museum, Cairo, CG 34183. For a translation, see Davies, *Egyptian Historical Records of the Later Eighteenth Dynasty*, Fascicle VI, 30–33.

22 On the tomb, see for example, Benderitter, 'Ay – TA 25'.

23 Dodson, *Amarna Sunset*, 65–67.

24 Dodson, *Amarna Sunset*, 79.

25 For Maya's career, see: Kawai, *Studies in the Reign of Tutankhamun*, 322–334.

26 For Userhat-Hatiay's career, see: Kawai, *Studies in the Reign of Tutankhamun*, 370–376.

27 This statue is in the Egyptian Museum, Cairo, CG 42052. See Eaton-Krauss, *The Unknown Tutankhamun*, 50–51.

28 Kawai, *Studies in the Reign of Tutankhamun*, 468.

29 On the name change and the tomb, see Kawai, *Studies in the Reign of Tutankhamun*, 462–464.

30 Kawai, *Studies in the Reign of Tutankhamun*, 482–485.

31 Kawai, *Studies in the Reign of Tutankhamun*, 501–503.

32 Kawai, *Studies in the Reign of Tutankhamun*, 490–496.

33 Stevens, 'Death and the City', 111.

34 This is KV 55 in the Valley of the Kings. Theban Mapping Project, 'KV 55: Tiye (?) or Akhenaten (?)', https://thebanmappingproject.com/index.php/tombs/kv-55-tiye-or-akhenaten. For an overview of the tomb and its burial equipment, see Kawai, *Studies in the Reign of Tutankhamun*, 236–239.

35 Although archaeologists once believed the body in the coffin to be Smenkhkare, it is now thought more likely to be Akhenaten. For an overview of the investigations into the skeleton in KV 55, including the arguments regarding whether the body should be identified as Akhenaten or Smenkhkare, see, for example, Filer, 'The KV 55 Body: The Facts'; Hawass and Saleem, *Scanning the Pharaohs*, 84–87.

36 Kawai, *Studies in the Reign of Tutankhamun*, 236–239.

37 Kawai, *Studies in the Reign of Tutankhamun*, 121 and 230–232.

38 The coffins and hair are Carter nos 320b, d, e.

39 The fake, smaller leopard skin with fake head is Carter no. 21t; the larger, true leopard skin with a fake head is Carter no. 44q. Vogelsang-Eastwood, *Tutankhamun's Wardrobe*, 104–108.

40 Kawai, 'Ay Versus Horemheb', 265.

41 The foldable bed is Carter no. 586. The foldable headrest is Carter no. 403d. See Reeves, *The Complete Tutankhamun*, 182–183.

42 This canopy reconstruction is based on a canopy now known to be part of one of Tutankhamun's chariots. See Kawai et al., 'The Ceremonial Canopied Chariot of Tutankhamun (JE61990 and JE60705)'; also, see Brock, 'A Possible Chariot Canopy for Tutankhamun', 29–43; Reeves, *The Complete Tutankhamun*, 187. The collapsible canopy is Carter no. 123. The stool with cushion is Carter no. 511.

43 Carter no. 50a. Vogelsang-Eastwood, *Tutankhamun's Wardrobe*, 41; Nomura and Rinaldo, *The Weavers of Tutankhamun*, 21–25; Vogelsang-Eastwood, *Pharaonic Egyptian Clothing*, 138–139.

44 This staff is Carter no. 229. See Reeves, *The Complete Tutankhamun*, 178.

45 The following reconstruction is based on carvings at Luxor Temple. See: Epigraphic Survey, *Reliefs and Inscriptions at Luxor Temple*, vol. 1.

46 Epigraphic Survey, *Reliefs and Inscriptions at Luxor Temple*, vol. 1, 15.

47 For a plan of the temple, explaining its sectors and when they were constructed, see Bell, 'The New Kingdom "Divine" Temple', 149.

48 For this reconstruction of events, based on the architecture and decoration at Luxor Temple, see Bell, 'The New Kingdom "Divine" Temple', 173–174.

49 Epigraphic Survey, *Reliefs and Inscriptions at Luxor Temple*, vol. 1, 82, 83; Kawai, *Studies in the Reign of Tutankhamun*, 43. Bell, 'The New Kingdom "Divine" Temple', 153.

50 Darnell and Manassa, *Tutankhamun's Armies*, 183.

51 Carter no. 367j. Also see Nomura and Rinaldo, *The Weavers of Tutankhamun*, 26.

52 Darnell and Manassa, *Tutankhamun's Armies*, 183. For the scene, see the second court, west wall, in Benderitter, 'Horemheb – Saqqara'.

53 Amarna Letter EA 9. See: Bryce, *Letters of the Great Kings*, 76.

54 Darnell and Manassa, *Tutankhamun's Armies*, 109–110.

55 Darnell and Manassa, *Tutankhamun's Armies*, 121. Scenes of Nubian prisoners are also found in Horemheb's Saqqara tomb, see second court, east wall, in Benderitter, 'Horemheb – Saqqara'.

56 Darnell and Manassa, *Tutankhamun's Armies*, 107.

57 Based on scenes in Huy's Theban Tomb, TT 40. See Benderitter, 'Huy – TT 40', 2.

58 These scenes are found in Huy's tomb at Thebes, TT 40. See Benderitter, 'Huy – TT 40', 3; and Darnell and Manassa, *Tutankhamun's Armies*, 127–131.

59 Shaw, *War and Trade with the Pharaohs*, 107.

3. THE MORTAL GOD

1   For Tutankhamun's rest house at Giza, see Kemp, *Ancient Egypt*, second edition, 282–284.

2   For a translation of this stele, see Cumming, *Egyptian Historical Records of the Later Eighteenth Dynasty*, Fascicle III, 247–251.

3   Kawai, *Studies in the Reign of Tutankhamun*, 307–308.

4   Kawai, *Studies in the Reign of Tutankhamun*, 407–410.

5   Kawai, *Studies in the Reign of Tutankhamun*, 350–353.

6   Kawai, *Studies in the Reign of Tutankhamun*, 411–417.

7   For these palace officials, see Kawai, *Studies in the Reign of Tutankhamun*, 417–418 (Panehesy), 422–423 (Mahy), 423–425 (Iny) and 430 (Tjay).

8   Vogelsang-Eastwood, *Tutankhamun's Wardrobe*, 15, 18–19, 48–50; Vogelsang-Eastwood, *Pharaonic Egyptian Clothing*, 11. Also see Shaw, *The Pharaoh*, 75–78. For examples of Tutankhamun's loincloths, see Carter no. 50b. Although the individuals who managed Tutankhamun's wardrobe, crowns and loincloths are not known, these offices are attested under other kings' reigns.

9   Carter no. 367i. Nomura and Rinaldo, *The Weavers of Tutankhamun*, 26; Vogelsang-Eastwood, *Tutankhamun's Wardrobe*, 58.

10 Veldmeijer, *Tutankhamun's Footwear*, 139–142.

11 Shaw, *The Pharaoh*, 73.

12 For the box of shaving equipment, see Carter no. 68, and for a razor, see Carter no. 620:53; see Reeves, *The Complete Tutankhamun*, 159. Also see Davies, 'Tut'ankhamūn's Razor-Box: A Problem in Lexicography'.

13 Carter no. 269b and 271c-d. Reeves, *The Complete Tutankhamun*, 159.

14 Carter no. 256:40. See, for example, Reeves, *The Complete Tutankhamun*, 154. Also see Shaw, *The Pharaoh*, 75–78.

15 See kohl tube, Carter no. 46jj, for example, and kohl sticks found in box Carter no. 44. Reeves, *The Complete Tutankhamun*, 158.

16 On Tutankhamun's stone vessels, see Reeves, *The Complete Tutankhamun*, 198–199.

17 Carter no. 210.

18 Carter no. 584.

19 Although the solar calendar and Egypt's civil calendar were normally out of alignment due to the latter being slightly shorter than a true solar year, roughly at the time of Tutankhamun's reign, the two were aligned. This means that the heliacal rising of Sirius, which marked the start of Egypt's solar new year, aligned with the civil calendar new year. See Depuydt, *Civil Calendar and Lunar Calendar*

in Ancient Egypt, 17; Fukaya, *The Festivals of Opet, the Valley, and the New Year*, 8.

20 Fukaya, *The Festivals of Opet, the Valley, and the New Year*, 111.

21 Fukaya, *The Festivals of Opet, the Valley, and the New Year*, 114.

22 Fukaya, *The Festivals of Opet, the Valley, and the New Year*, 89–91.

23 Fukaya, *The Festivals of Opet, the Valley, and the New Year*, 121.

24 Fukaya, *The Festivals of Opet, the Valley, and the New Year*, 80–81.

25 Fukaya, *The Festivals of Opet, the Valley, and the New Year*, 94.

26 Fukaya, *The Festivals of Opet, the Valley, and the New Year*, 84.

27 Fukaya, *The Festivals of Opet, the Valley, and the New Year*, 81.

28 Davies, *The Tomb of Ken-Amun at Thebes*, 24.

29 On the location where kings received their new year gifts, see Fukaya, *The Festivals of Opet, the Valley, and the New Year*, 107–110.

30 Fukaya, *The Festivals of Opet, the Valley, and the New Year*, 109.

31 Brown, 'Tutankhamun's Sticks'; Davies, *The Tomb of Ken-Amun at Thebes*, 28.

32 Based on gifts given to other kings at the new year festival. See Fukaya, *The Festivals of Opet, the Valley, and the New Year*, 120–121; Säve-Söderbergh, *Four Eighteenth Dynasty Tombs*, 3–8, pls I–VI and IXa; Davies, *The Tomb of Ken-Amun at Thebes*, 25–31.

33 Fukaya, *The Festivals of Opet, the Valley, and the New Year*, 126; Davies, *The Tomb of Ken-Amun at Thebes*, 24.

34 Carter no. 50j. Nomura and Rinaldo, *The Weavers of Tutankhamun*, 21–25.

35 Carter no. 21ff. Vogelsang-Eastwood, *Tutankhamun's Wardrobe*, 59.

36 Carter no. 256ppp. This pectoral shows signs of use, see Reeves, *The Complete Tutankhamun*, 152.

37 Carter no. 256qq.

38 Carter no. 269a(5).

39 Lacovara, *The World of Ancient Egypt*, 173; Veldmeijer, *Tutankhamun's Footwear*, 10.

40 For food items in Tutankhamun's tomb, see: Reeves, *The Complete Tutankhamun*, 205–207; Guasch Jané, 'Food', 179.

41 Based on a scene from the Little Golden Shrine found in Tutankhamun's tomb (Carter no. 108): Griffith Institute, http://www.griffith.ox.ac.uk/gri/carter/108-p0314a.html.

42 For royal banquets, see Shaw, *The Pharaoh*, 101–103 and 106–107.

43 See the image of Tutankhamun at bottom right of Reeves, *The Complete Tutankhamun*, 29.

44 Guasch Jané, 'The Meaning of Wine in Egyptian Tombs', 853.

45 Guasch Jané, 'The Meaning of Wine in Egyptian Tombs', 853.

46 See scene from the tomb of Nebamun, Shaw, *The Pharaoh*, 107.

47 Carter no. 585r. For a detailed description, see Tait, *Game-boxes and Accessories from the Tomb of Tutankhamun*, 17–19. The other box is Carter no. 393. For the games, see: Reeves, *The Complete Tutankhamun*, 160–162.

48 King Ramesses III had himself depicted playing senet with harem women at Medinet Habu.

49 See bed, Carter no. 466. Reeves, *The Complete Tutankhamun*, 181.

50 Shaw, *The Egyptian Myths*, 148–149.

51 Carter no. 403d.

52 Reconstruction based on the decoration of various palaces. Shaw, 'Palaces', 398–399; Shaw, *The Pharaoh*, 70–72, 80–83 and 144–145.

53 For the dating of this event, see: Dodson, 'The Canopic Equipment from the Serapeum of Memphis', 62.

54 According to the Greek writer Herodotus in the fifth century BC. See Dodson, 'Bull Cults', 72–73.

55 Dodson, 'Bull Cults', 72.

56 Basing the burial under Tutankhamun on that made under Amenhotep III. Dodson, 'Bull Cults', 76.

57 These are now in the Louvre. See Dodson, 'The Canopic Equipment from the Serapeum of Memphis', 62.

58 See Eaton-Krauss, *The Unknown Tutankhamun*, 82.

59 Carter no. 2690. Eaton-Krauss, *The Unknown Tutankhamun*, 82. Hellinckx, 'Tutankhamun's So-called Stole', 15.

60 See Eaton-Krauss, *The Unknown Tutankhamun*, 82.

61 This campaign appears to have happened towards the end of Tutankhamun's life. See Bryce, *The Kingdom of the Hittites*, 177–183; Bryce, 'The Death of Niphururiya and Its Aftermath', 104.

62 This is perhaps obliquely referred to in Tutankhamun's Restoration Stele, when he mentions that Egypt's armies failed when sent out. Also, see Shaw, *War and Trade with the Pharaohs*, 101–102.

63 Carter no. 587a.

64 For a description of Qadesh and its surroundings, see Kitchen, *Pharaoh Triumphant*, 54.

65 On military camps, see: Shaw, *War and Trade with the Pharaohs*, 81–82; Shaw, *The Pharaoh*, 128–129.

66 Assuming that the unidentified prisoner in the cage is Aitakama, which appears likely. Darnell and Manassa, *Tutankhamun's Armies*, 182.

67 A good account of these scenes, and where they originate, can be found in Darnell and Manassa, *Tutankhamun's Armies*, 178–184.

68 Shaw, *War and Trade with the Pharaohs*, 106.

69 Eaton-Krauss, *The Unknown Tutankhamun*, 80–81.

70 For these scenes, from Horemheb's Saqqara tomb, see Benderitter, 'Horemheb – Saqqara'. Also, Ghaly and Ibrahim, 'Reward Ceremony Scenes in Private Tombs of Post-Amarna Period in Thebes and Memphis', 170–172.

71 Based on a scene from the Little Golden Shrine found in Tutankhamun's tomb (Carter no. 108): Griffith Institute, http://www.griffith.ox.ac.uk/gri/carter/108-p1551.html.

72 Carter no. 48i(1). McLeod, *Composite Bows from the Tomb of Tutankhamun*, 12–14.

73 Carter no. 335. McLeod, *Self Bows and Other Archery Tackle from the Tomb of Tutankhamun*, 26–38 and 44–49.

74 Based on a scene from the Little Golden Shrine found in Tutankhamun's tomb (Carter no. 108): see Reeves, *The Complete Tutankhamun*, 140.

75 Carter no. 242. Reeves, *The Complete Tutankhamun*, 179.

76 Strouhal, *Life of the Ancient Egyptians*, 122.

77 For hunting animals in the desert, see Strouhal, *Life of the Ancient Egyptians*, 119–120.

78 For the weapons, see Reeves, *The Complete Tutankhamun*, 174–177.

79 Carter no. 620:52. See Reeves, *The Complete Tutankhamun*, 177.

80 Found in a box in the tomb. For the box, see Carter no. 585.

81 The scale armour is Carter no. 587 – the same number as the box in which Carter found it. See Reeves, *The Complete Tutankhamun*, 176.

82 Shaw, *The Pharaoh*, 113.

83 The chariots from Tutankhamun's tomb reflect his love of riding. Of the six found, chariots A4 and A5 show signs that they were used. See: Crouwel, 'Studying the Six Chariots from the Tomb of Tutankhamun – An Update', 85; Littauer and Crouwel, *Chariots and Related Equipment from the Tomb of Tutankhamun*, 100.

84 Carter no. 21. See Carter and Mace, *The Tomb of Tut.Ankh.Amen*, vol. 1, 161–162.

85 Carter, *The Tomb of Tut.Ankh.Amen*, vol. 2, 58–59.

86 Eaton-Krauss, *The Unknown Tutankhamun*, 99–100.

87 My reconstruction of Tutankhamun's death is based on the recent arguments of, and possible scenario suggested by, Hawass and Saleem, *Scanning the Pharaohs*, 96–97 and 102–103.

88 Allen, *The Art of Medicine in Ancient Egypt*, 11.

89 Allen, *The Art of Medicine in Ancient Egypt*, 11–12.

90 Tutankhamun was infected with more than one strain of malaria.

Hawass et al., 'Ancestry and Pathology in King Tutankhamun's Family'; Hawass and Saleem, *Scanning the Pharaohs*, 102–103.

91 The Edwin Smith Papyrus covers a number of medical problems, including those classed as orthopaedic; sadly, it doesn't contain the content for the legs. See: Blomstedt, 'Orthopedic Surgery in Ancient Egypt', 671.

92 On the medical use of honey, see Allen, *The Art of Medicine in Ancient Egypt*, 42. For demons being repulsed by honey, see Shaw, *The Egyptian Myths*, 156.

93 Bogensperger, 'Alum in Ancient Egypt', 257–258.

94 My reconstruction is based on how doctors treated a fractured humerus. See: Allen, *The Art of Medicine in Ancient Egypt*, 95; Brorson, 'Management of Fractures of the Humerus in Ancient Egypt, Greece, and Rome. An Historical Review', 1908; Blomstedt, 'Orthopedic Surgery in Ancient Egypt', 671–672.

95 For Tutankhamun's age at death, see Hawass and Saleem, *Scanning the Pharaohs*, 94.

4. PREPARING FOR A JOURNEY

1 For the following events and their timings, see Bryce, *Letters of the Great Kings of the Ancient Near East*, 178–189; Bryce, 'The Death of Niphururiya and Its Aftermath', 97–105; Dodson, *Amarna Sunset*, 89–94.

2 Although Tutankhamun's tomb is the only royal burial from this era found relatively intact, the remains of artefacts from earlier and later kings' tombs reflect the same items. Objects that we recognize from the tomb also decorate one of the walls in the Tomb of King Seti II.

3 For these items, see Eaton-Krauss, *The Unknown Tutankhamun*, 106–107. The small gold coffins are Carter no. 266g 1–4; the pectoral is Carter no. 261p(1).

4 Following the arguments of Reeves, 'The Gold Mask of Ankhkheperure Neferneferuaten', 77–79; and Reeves, 'Tutankhamun's Mask Reconsidered', 511–526.

5 Laboury, 'The Artist Who Created the Most Famous Funerary Mask in the World?', 76.

6 For the sarcophagus, see Eaton-Krauss, *The Unknown Tutankhamun*, 88–92. It is also possible that it was adapted for Tutankhamun before his death.

7 For the theories regarding the sarcophagus, see Eaton-Krauss, *The Unknown Tutankhamun*, 88–92.

8   Eaton-Krauss, *The Unknown Tutankhamun*, 88–89.

9   The vessels are Carter nos 404 and 410; the scarab is Carter no. 1a; and the persea fruit is Carter no. 585u. See Harris, 'Akhenaten and Nefernefruaten in the Tomb of Tut'ankhamūn', 55–56.

10   The coffins and hair are Carter nos 320b,d,e. Harris, 'Akhenaten and Nefernefruaten in the Tomb of Tut'ankhamūn', 56.

11   The clappers are Carter no. 620(13); see Manniche, *Musical Instruments from the Tomb of Tutankhamun*, 3–4. The scribal palette is Carter no. 262. Harris, 'Akhenaten and Nefernefruaten in the Tomb of Tut'ankhamūn', 56.

12   The skullcap is Carter no. 256tttt. See: Harris, 'Akhenaten and Nefernefruaten in the Tomb of Tut'ankhamūn', 57. Kawai, *Studies in the Reign of Tutankhamun*, 23 and 108.

13   The plain box is Carter no. 317, and the mummies within are Carter nos 317a and 317b. See Hawass and Saleem, *Scanning the Pharaohs*, 107.

14   Marchant, *The Shadow King*, 77.

15   The shabti is Carter no. 318b, and the small bier is Carter no. 331a.

16   Carter nos 318a, 318c, 330i, 330j, 330k. Kawai, *Studies in the Reign of Tutankhamun*, 114.

17   Carter no. 490. Černý, *Hieratic Inscriptions from the Tomb of Tutankhamun*, 4.

18   Černý, *Hieratic Inscriptions from the Tomb of Tutankhamun*, 9, 14, 16–17.

19   Carter, *The Tomb of Tut.Ankh.Amen*, vol. 3, 52–56.

20   On the earlier creation of some of these statuettes, including the statuette of the king standing on a leopard (Carter no. 289b), see Eaton-Krauss, *The Unknown Tutankhamun*, 108–109.

21   Eaton-Krauss, *The Unknown Tutankhamun*, 108.

22   Carter, *The Tomb of Tut.Ankh.Amen*, vol. 3, 51–52.

23   Eaton-Krauss, *The Unknown Tutankhamun*, 109.

24   Kawai, *Studies in the Reign of Tutankhamun*, 331.

25   Kawai, *Studies in the Reign of Tutankhamun*, 375.

26   The tomb eventually used by Aye was perhaps originally intended for Tutankhamun. See Kawai, *Studies in the Reign of Tutankhamun*, 118–119.

27   On the probable original appearance of the tomb, see Kawai, *Studies in the Reign of Tutankhamun*, 117–118.

28   See Austin, 'The Cost of a Commute'; Shaw, 'Steep Commute Gave Ancient Egyptian Workers Osteoarthritis', https://www.science.org/content/article/steep-commute-gave-ancient-egyptian-workers-osteoarthritis.

29   Kawai, *Studies in the Reign of Tutankhamun*, 118.

30 Lowe, 'Tomb Recording: Epigraphy, Photography, Digital Imaging, and 3D Surveys', 532. Robins, 'The Decorative Program in the Tomb of Tutankhamun (KV 62)', 322. For digging tombs, see Theban Mapping Project, 'Tomb Digging and Cutting Techniques', https://thebanmapping project.com/articles/tomb-digging-and-cutting-techniques.

31 Hays, 'Funerary Rituals (Pharaonic Period)', 4–5.

32 Hays, 'Funerary Rituals (Pharaonic Period)', 5.

33 Leek, *The Human Remains from the Tomb of Tutankhamun*, 15 and 17.

34 Ikram, 'Some Thoughts on the Mummification of King Tutankhamun', 293–298. Rühli and Ikram, 'Purported Medical Diagnoses of Pharaoh Tutankhamun, c. 1325 BC-', 53.

35 The heart might have been accidentally pulled out in modern times. The king is also missing some of his ribs, vertebrae, and sternum, though this could have been caused by looters disturbing the body, probably during the Second World War. See Ikram, 'Some Thoughts on the Mummification of King Tutankhamun', 295–298; Rühli and Ikram, 'Purported Medical Diagnoses of Pharaoh Tutankhamun, c. 1325 BC-', 58; Harer, 'New Evidence for King Tutankhamen's Death', 228–233; Forbes, Ikram, and Kamrin, 'Tutankhamen's Missing Ribs'.

36 See Desroches-Noblecourt, *Tutankhamen*, 223, image 133.

37 Desroches-Noblecourt, *Tutankhamen*, 222, 223–224. Harer, 'New Evidence for King Tutankhamen's Death', 231; Leek, *The Human Remains from the Tomb of Tutankhamun*, 14.

38 This is an unusual position, because kings' arms were usually crossed diagonally across the chest. Salima Ikram has argued that Tutankhamun's covering of black resin, his erect penis, and the position of his arms, among other evidence, might have been to make the body appear more like the god Osiris. Ikram, 'Some Thoughts on the Mummification of King Tutankhamun', 292–301.

39 Rühli and Ikram, 'Purported Medical Diagnoses of Pharaoh Tutankhamun, c. 1325 BC-', 53; Ikram, 'Some Thoughts on the Mummification of King Tutankhamun', 294, 298–301.

40 Ikram, 'Some Thoughts on the Mummification of King Tutankhamun', 297–298. However, two heart scarabs as necklaces were found on Tutankhamun's body. See Carter nos 256a and 256q.

41 Desroches-Noblecourt, *Tutankhamen*, 222.

42 See Desroches-Noblecourt, *Tutankhamen*, 232, image 143 for the rings, and 231, image 142 for the bracelets.

43 The dagger with a meteoritic blade is Carter no. 256k. See: Comelli et al., 'The Meteoritic Origin of Tutankhamun's Iron Dagger Blade',

1301–1309. Also see Matsui et al., 'The Manufacture and Origin of the Tutankhamen Meteoritic Iron Dagger'.

44 Desroches-Noblecourt, *Tutankhamen*, 224–226.

45 Hays, 'Funerary Rituals (Pharaonic Period)', 6.

46 Winlock and Arnold, *Tutankhamun's Funeral*, 12.

47 For the following events, and their timings, see Bryce, *Letters of the Great Kings of the Ancient Near East*, 178–188.

48 Bryce, *The Kingdom of the Hittites*, 154.

49 Bryce, *Life and Society in the Hittite World*, 232.

50 Bryce, 'The Death of Niphururiya and Its Aftermath', 99.

51 Bryce, 'The Death of Niphururiya and Its Aftermath', 100; Bryce, *Letters of the Great Kings of the Ancient Near East*, 188.

52 For a brief account of these events, see Shaw, *War and Trade with the Pharaohs*, 107–108.

53 Robins, 'The Decorative Program in the Tomb of Tutankhamun (KV 62)', 321 and 331; Robins, *The Art of Ancient Egypt*, 158.

54 For the tomb's decoration, see: Robins, 'The Decorative Program in the Tomb of Tutankhamun (KV 62)', 321–341; Benderitter, 'Tutankhamun – KV 62'; Reeves, *The Complete Tutankhamun*, 72–74.

55 Lowe, 'Tomb Recording: Epigraphy, Photography, Digital Imaging, and 3D Surveys', 533. This scene is unique in a royal tomb – perhaps the expected arrival of a foreign prince as pharaoh necessitated the extra emphasis on legitimacy.

56 Robins, 'The Decorative Program in the Tomb of Tutankhamun (KV 62)', 322.

57 Robins, 'The Decorative Program in the Tomb of Tutankhamun (KV 62)', 322.

58 Kawai, *Studies in the Reign of Tutankhamun*, 117–118.

59 For food items in Tutankhamun's tomb, see: Reeves, *The Complete Tutankhamun*, 205–207; Guasch Jané, 'Food', 179.

60 Černý, *Hieratic Inscriptions from the Tomb of Tutankhamun*, 6–7.

61 Černý, *Hieratic Inscriptions from the Tomb of Tutankhamun*, 18.

62 Reeves, *The Complete Tutankhamun*, 207.

63 Carter no. 563. Černý, *Hieratic Inscriptions from the Tomb of Tutankhamun*, 3–4.

64 Reeves, *The Complete Tutankhamun*, 205. Carter, *The Tomb of Tut.Ankh. Amen*, vol. 3, 61.

65 Desroches-Noblecourt, *Tutankhamen*, 237.

66 McLeod, *Self Bows and other Archery Tackle from the Tomb of Tutankhamun*, 64.

67 For Horemheb's probable presence at the funeral, see Kawai, 'Ay Versus Horemheb', 271–273. Horemheb might be one of the figures shown in the funeral procession depicted in Tutankhamun's tomb, see Robins, 'The Decorative Program in the Tomb of Tutankhamun (KV 62)', 324.

68 Hays, 'Funerary Rituals (Pharaonic Period)', 6.

69 Desroches-Noblecourt, *Tutankhamen*, 237.

70 Winlock and Arnold, *Tutankhamun's Funeral*, 12.

71 Winlock and Arnold, *Tutankhamun's Funeral*, 12–13.

72 Hays, 'Funerary Rituals (Pharaonic Period)', 7.

73 For this possibility, see Reeves, 'Tutankhamun's Mask Reconsidered', 515.

74 Edwards, *Tutankhamun: His Tomb and Its Treasures*; Carter, *The Tomb of Tut.Ankh.Amen*, vol. 2, 121–151.

75 Carter no. 266b.

76 Carter no. 266a.

77 Carter no. 108. Reeves, *The Complete Tutankhamun*, 140–141.

78 Carter no. 261.

79 The sash is Carter no. 261d. The tunic is Carter no. 261a. See Vogelsang-Eastwood, *Tutankhamun's Wardrobe*, 26, 54–55.

80 Carter, *The Tomb of Tut.Ankh.Amen*, vol. 3, 41–42.

81 The wooden cow head is Carter no. 264. See Carter, *The Tomb of Tut. Ankh.Amen*, vol. 3, 46.

82 Shaw, *Egyptian Mythology*, 161 and 164.

83 Here I'm assuming that the lid broke during the burial. For the break in the sarcophagus lid, see Eaton-Krauss, 'Tutankhamun's Sarcophagus: An Addition and Two Corrections', 218; Eaton-Krauss, *The Unknown Tutankhamun*, 115. Carter, *Tut.Ankh.Amen*, vol. 2, 99.

84 Eaton-Krauss, *The Unknown Tutankhamun*, 158, note 70.

85 Eaton-Krauss, *The Unknown Tutankhamun*, 115–117 and 158 note 73; Desroches-Noblecourt, *Tutankhamen*, 76; Guasch Jané, 'About the Orientation of the Magical Bricks in Tutankhamun's Burial Chamber', 113–114.

86 Eaton-Krauss, *The Unknown Tutankhamun*, 115.

87 Carter, *The Tomb of Tut.Ankh.Amen*, vol. 2, 91 and 96–97.

88 Carter, *The Tomb of Tut.Ankh.Amen*, vol. 2, 94–95.

89 Carter, *The Tomb of Tut.Ankh.Amen*, vol. 2, 92.

90 On the timing of these events, see Carter, *The Tomb of Tut.Ankh.Amen*, vol. 2, 70.

91 For the decoration of this wall, see Reeves, *The Complete Tutankhamun*, 73–74.

92 Robins, 'The Decorative Program in the Tomb of Tutankhamun (KV 62)', 321 and 331; Robins, *The Art of Ancient Egypt*, 158.

93 Guasch Jané, 'About the Orientation of the Magical Bricks in Tutankhamun's Burial Chamber', 118.

94 For the seals, see Cross, 'The Re-Sealing of KV62', 16–17.

95 The pit is now KV 54. See Winlock and Arnold, *Tutankhamun's Funeral*, 16–17.

5. THE DARK BEFORE THE DAWN

1 Dodson, *Amarna Sunset*, 100; Murnane, *The Road to Kadesh*, 25–28.

2 Dodson, *Amarna Sunset*, 102–104.

3 This tomb is KV 55 in the Valley of the Kings. For the timing of the re-entry and defacement of the coffin, see Dodson and Cross, 'The Valley of the Kings in the Reign of Tutankhamun'. Here, I'm assuming that the coffin and body within belonged to Akhenaten, although scholars also argue that it could be Smenkhkare. For an overview of the investigations into the skeleton in KV 55, including the arguments regarding whether the body should be identified as Akhenaten or Smenkhkare, see, for example, Filer, 'The KV 55 Body: The Facts'; Hawass and Saleem, *Scanning the Pharaohs*, 84–87.

4 Goelet, 'Tomb Robberies in the Valley of the Kings', 452.

5 This is Carter no. 435. See Reeves, *The Complete Tutankhamun*, 97.

6 For a photo of the doorway to the annexe beneath the couch, see Reeves, *The Complete Tutankhamun*, 146.

7 For the first tomb robbery, see Reeves, *The Complete Tutankhamun*, 95–96.

8 Goelet, 'Tomb Robberies in the Valley of the Kings', 451.

9 Černý, *Hieratic Inscriptions from the Tomb of Tutankhamun*, vii.

10 For the second tomb robbery, see Reeves, *The Complete Tutankhamun*, 96–97.

11 The linen is Carter no. 44b. It was probably an item of Tutankhamun's clothing, see Vogelsang-Eastwood, *Tutankhamun's Wardrobe*, 62–63.

12 Carter no. 620(122), accidentally also given Carter no. 620(116). Černý, *Hieratic Inscriptions from the Tomb of Tutankhamun*, 7.

13 On such floods, and that they could reach two metres in depth in the Valley of the Kings, see Harrell, 'Violence in Earth, Water, and Sky', 250–251.

14 See Cross, 'The Re-Sealing of KV62', 18; and Cross, 'The Hydrology of the Valley of the Kings'.

15 Dodson and Hilton, *The Complete Royal Families of Ancient Egypt*, 151–153.

16 For the tomb decoration, see Benderitter, 'Ay – KV 23', 2.

17 For this, see Dodson, *Amarna Sunset*, 105–106.

18 For a recent translation of Horemheb's coronation text, see: Bryson, *The Reign of Horemheb*, 158–166.

19 For a summary of the Horemheb Edict – inscribed on a stele at the Temple of Amun at Karnak – see Wilkinson, *The Rise and Fall of Ancient Egypt*, 313–314; also see Booth, *Horemheb: The Forgotten Pharaoh*, 116–120.

20 Kawai, *Studies in the Reign of Tutankhamun*, 503.

21 For an overview of the campaigns of Horemheb and trade with Punt, see Booth, *Horemheb: The Forgotten Pharaoh*, 121–123.

22 The extra work meant that the tomb remained unfinished at Horemheb's death. Dodson, *The Royal Tombs of Ancient Egypt*, 44 (ebook edition).

23 For the remains of Horemheb's burial goods, see Booth, *Horemheb: The Forgotten Pharaoh*, 131–135.

24 For an example of an added uraeus, see photo 'View T 15' in the 'Statue Room' section in Benderitter, 'Horemheb – Saqqara', 1.

25 Dodson, *Amarna Sunset*, 115.

26 On Mutnodjmet, see for example, Bryson, *The Reign of Horemheb*, 52–54.

27 On the destruction of these kings' images and the tomb of Aye, see Eaton-Krauss, *The Unknown Tutankhamun*, 120–121; and Dodson, *Amarna Sunset*, 108.

28 Dodson, *Amarna Sunset*, 120–122.

29 For the removal of Ankhesenamun, see Eaton-Krauss, *The Unknown Tutankhamun*, 35–36.

30 Eaton-Krauss, *The Unknown Tutankhamun*, 79.

31 Eaton-Krauss, *The Unknown Tutankhamun*, 54.

32 For the family of King Ramesses I, see Kitchen, *Pharaoh Triumphant*, 16–18.

6. THE LOST TOMB

1 Baedeker, *Egypt and the Sudan*, 251.

2 Baedeker, *Egypt and the Sudan*, 252 and 281.

3 Baedeker, *Egypt and the Sudan*, 285.

4 Baedeker, *Egypt and the Sudan*, 318.

5 Shaw, 'Auguste Mariette', 59–60.

6 Tyldesley, *Egypt: How a Lost Civilization Was Rediscovered*, 183.

7 For a short overview of Howard Carter's life and career, see Shaw, 'Howard Carter', 100–105.

8 Naunton, *Egyptologists' Notebooks*, 202–204.

9 Shaw, 'Howard Carter', 102–103; Winstone, *Howard Carter*, 94–99.

10 Baedeker, *Egypt and the Sudan*, 251.

11 Winstone, *Howard Carter*, 104.

12 Marchant, *The Shadow King*, 30.

13 Winstone, *Howard Carter*, 102–105.

14 Reeves, *The Complete Tutankhamun*, 48–49.

15 Winstone, *Howard Carter*, 123.

16 For Carter's account of his evidence, see Carter and Mace, *The Tomb of Tut.Ankh.Amen*, vol. 1, 118–121.

17 This is known as KV 54.

18 This is known as KV 58.

19 Davis, *The Tombs of Harmhabi and Touatânkhamanou*, 2–3, where the date of the discovery of KV 58 is incorrectly given as 1907. Reeves and Wilkinson, *The Complete Valley of the Kings*, 126 (for KV 54) and 186 (for KV 58).

20 This is known as KV 55.

21 Romer, *Valley of the Kings*, 307.

22 Winstone, *Howard Carter*, 128 and 155 (on this latter page, the sum is instead cited as £40,000 over sixteen years).

23 Marchant, *The Shadow King*, 34–36.

24 The following sections are based on Howard Carter's 1922 diary and journal: Griffith Institute, http://www.griffith.ox.ac.uk/gri/4sea1not.html.

25 See: Griffith Institute, http://www.griffith.ox.ac.uk/gri/tut-files/Carter_041122.html.

26 Carter and Mace, *The Tomb of Tut.Ankh.Amen*, vol. 1, 142. This is as quoted in Carter's book describing the event. Other sources suggest that he used different words at the time. See, for example, Parkinson, *Tutankhamun: Excavating the Archive*, 21.

27 Based on before-and-after photographs, a letter from Lord Carnarvon to the Egyptologist Alan Gardiner, and the account of Mervyn Herbert, Lord Carnarvon's brother. See Reeves, *The Complete Tutankhamun*, 54–55 and 82. Also see the comments of Lucas, 'Notes on Some of the Objects from the Tomb of Tut-Ankhamun', 136.

28 Carter and Mace, *The Tomb of Tut.Ankh.Amen*, vol. 1, xv–xvi.

29 Carter and Mace, *The Tomb of Tut.Ankh.Amen*, vol. 1, xix.

30 Based on Lucas' notes: Griffith Institute, http://www.griffith.ox.ac.uk/discoveringTut/conservation/4lucasn1.html.

31 For Carter's 1923 diary and journal, see: Griffith Institute, http://www.griffith.ox.ac.uk/gri/4sea1no2.html.

32 Winstone, *Howard Carter*, 177.

33 Reeves, *The Complete Tutankhamun*, 82.

34 Reid, 'Remembering and Forgetting Tutankhamun', 160.
35 Reid, 'Remembering and Forgetting Tutankhamun', 160–161.
36 Riggs, *Treasured*, 83.
37 Winstone, *Howard Carter*, 170–176.
38 Riggs, *Treasured*, 92.
39 Carter, *The Tomb of Tut.Ankh.Amen*, vol. 2, xx; also see Fryxell, 'Tutankhamen, Egyptomania, and Temporal Enchantment in Interwar Britain', 523.
40 Baedeker, *Egypt and the Sudan*, 253.
41 Brier, *Egyptomania*, 169.
42 Brier, *Egyptomania*, 173.
43 Brier, *Egyptomania*, 173.
44 Fryxell, 'Tutankhamen, Egyptomania, and Temporal Enchantment in Interwar Britain', 525 and 527.
45 Brier, *Egyptomania*, 173.
46 The replicas are now kept in the Hands on History Museum in Hull. Museum Collections Hull, http://museumcollections.hullcc.gov.uk/collections/storydetail.php?irn=3&master=4; Fryxell, 'Tutankhamen, Egyptomania, and Temporal Enchantment in Interwar Britain', 530-532.
47 Fryxell, 'Tutankhamen, Egyptomania, and Temporal Enchantment in Interwar Britain', 523.
48 Fagan, *Lord and Pharaoh*, 134.
49 Winstone, *Howard Carter*, 181–185.
50 See Carter's diary entry: Griffith Institute, http://www.griffith.ox.ac.uk/gri/4sea1no2.html.
51 For a summary of these events, see Reeves, *The Complete Tutankhamun*, 62–63; and Winstone, *Howard Carter*, 185–188.
52 Winstone, *Howard Carter*, 187 and 189.
53 Winstone, *Howard Carter*, 190.
54 For the curse, see Winstone, *Howard Carter*, 190, 261–266; and Tyldesley, 'Tutankhamun: Who's Afraid of the Pharaoh's Curse?', https://www.historyextra.com/period/ancient-egypt/howard-carter-discovery-tutankhamun-tomb-lord-carnarvon-pharaoh-curse/.
55 Reeves, *The Complete Tutankhamun*, 63.
56 Carter, *The Tomb of Tut.Ankh.Amen*, vol. 2, xxiv–xxvi.
57 Fryxell, 'Tutankhamen, Egyptomania, and Temporal Enchantment in Interwar Britain', 533–535.
58 Tyldesley, 'Tutankhamun: Who's Afraid of the Pharaoh's Curse?', https://www.historyextra.com/period/ancient-egypt/howard-carter-discovery-tutankhamun-tomb-lord-carnarvon-pharaoh-curse/.

59 See Carter's diary entry: Griffith Institute, http://www.griffith.ox.ac. uk/gri/4sea1no2.html.

60 Reeves, *The Complete Tutankhamun*, 60.

61 Winstone, *Howard Carter*, 191.

62 Carter, *The Tomb of Tut.Ankh.Amen*, vol. 2, xi and xviii.

63 Marchant, *The Shadow King*, 57–58.

64 Winstone, *Howard Carter*, 209–212.

65 Riggs, *Treasured*, 73–74.

66 Riggs, *Treasured*, 100–101.

67 Marchant, *The Shadow King*, 59–60. Reeves, *The Complete Tutankhamun*, 64–66.

68 The following account is based on Carter's journal. Griffith Institute, http://www.griffith.ox.ac.uk/discoveringTut/journals-and-diaries/ season-4/journal.html.

69 Marchant, *The Shadow King*, 63.

70 Ikram, 'An Epistolary Footnote', 205–208.

71 For the autopsy and mummy, see: Carter, *The Tomb of Tut.Ankh.Amen*, vol. 2, 173–210; Derry in Carter, *The Tomb of Tut.Ankh.Amen*, vol. 2, 213–232; Leek, *The Human Remains from the Tomb of Tutankhamun*, 3–20; Carter's journal for 11–19 November 1925: Griffith Institute, http://www. griffith.ox.ac.uk/discoveringTut/journals-and-diaries/season-4/journal. html; and Marchant, *The Shadow King*, 63–74.

72 Leek, *The Human Remains from the Tomb of Tutankhamun*, 11.

73 Leek, *The Human Remains from the Tomb of Tutankhamun*, 11.

74 Leek, *The Human Remains from the Tomb of Tutankhamun*, 11–12.

75 Marchant, *The Shadow King*, 67.

76 Leek, *The Human Remains from the Tomb of Tutankhamun*, 12 and 18; Marchant, *The Shadow King*, 70; for the process, including removal of the hands, see Burton's photographs at the Griffith Institute, http:// www.griffith.ox.ac.uk/gri/carter/gallery/gal-039.html and http://www. griffith.ox.ac.uk/gri/carter/gallery/gal-040.html.

77 Leek, *The Human Remains from the Tomb of Tutankhamun*, 7; Hawass and Saleem, *Scanning the Pharaohs*, 90–91.

78 Romer, *Valley of the Kings*, 334; Marchant, *The Shadow King*, 71.

7. A CENTURY OF TUT-MANIA

1 Carter's journal entry for 27 November 1925: Griffith Institute, http:// www.griffith.ox.ac.uk/discoveringTut/journals-and-diaries/season-4/ journal.html. Also see Marchant, *The Shadow King*, 73.

2   Riggs, *Treasured*, 271.

3   Reid, 'Remembering and Forgetting Tutankhamun', 165.

4   Riggs, *Treasured*, 271–272.

5   Marchant, *The Shadow King*, 73–74; Riggs, *Treasured*, 272.

6   The final parts of the gilded shrines were removed from the tomb between 5 and 10 November 1930. See Carter's journal entry, Griffith Institute, http://www.griffith.ox.ac.uk/discoveringTut/journals-and-diaries/season-9/journal.html.

7   Winstone, *Howard Carter*, 286, 289 and 291.

8   Riggs, *Treasured*, 122.

9   Marchant, *The Shadow King*, 95–99, 106–107; Riggs, *Treasured*, 273–276; Forbes, Ikram and Kamrin, 'Tutankhamen's Missing Ribs', 50–56.

10 Marchant, *The Shadow King*, 120. Forbes, Ikram and Kamrin, 'Tutankhamen's Missing Ribs', 51 and 55.

11 Marchant, *The Shadow King*, 151–156; Riggs, *Treasured*, 284–286; Hawass and Saleem, *Scanning the Pharaohs*, 92–93.

12 Marchant, *The Shadow King*, 181–182.

13 Marchant, *The Shadow King*, 183–184. Hawass et al., 'Ancestry and Pathology in King Tutankhamun's Family'.

14 For a study of the various illnesses and physical problems assigned to Tutankhamun over the years, see Rühli and Ikram, 'Purported Medical Diagnoses of Pharaoh Tutankhamun, c. 1325 BC-', 52–63.

15 Veldmeijer and Ikram, 'Tutankhamun's Sticks and Staves', 12.

16 Rühli and Ikram, 'Purported Medical Diagnoses of Pharaoh Tutankhamun, c. 1325 BC-', 56.

17 For Harrison's notes, and an analysis of what they could mean for the recent investigation's conclusions, see the comments of Marchant, *The Shadow King*, 234–235.

18 Rühli and Ikram, 'Purported Medical Diagnoses of Pharaoh Tutankhamun, c. 1325 BC-', 57–59.

19 Hawass et al., 'Ancestry and Pathology in King Tutankhamun's Family'; Hawass and Saleem, *Scanning the Pharaohs*, 96–97 and 102–103.

20 Harer, 'New Evidence for King Tutankhamen's Death: His Bizarre Embalming', 228–233.

21 Ikram, 'Some Thoughts on the Mummification of King Tutankhamun', 295–296.

22 Riggs, *Treasured*, 158–163.

23 Riggs, *Treasured*, 250–251.

24 Riggs, *Treasured*, 252; Marchant, *The Shadow King*, 122–123.

25 McAlister, *Epic Encounters*, 125.

26 El-Aref, 'In Photos: Tutankhamun Artefacts to Go on Display at Hurghada, Sharm Museums', https://english.ahram.org.eg/NewsContent/9/40/378777/Antiquities/Ancient-Egypt/In-Photos-Tutankhamun-artefacts-to-go-on-display-a.aspx.

27 Schulze, 'Tutankhamun in West Germany, 1980–81', 53.

28 El-Aref, 'Tutankhamun's Gold Mask Restored After Botched Repair', https://english.ahram.org.eg/NewsContent/9/40/173700/Antiquities/Ancient-Egypt/Tutankhamuns-gold-mask-restored-after-botched-repa.aspx.

29 Hull Museums Collections, 'The Tutankhamun Replicas at Hull Museums', http://museumcollections.hullcc.gov.uk/collections/subtheme.php?irn=4.

30 Semmel Exhibitions, 'Partner Brochure for Tutankhamun: His Tomb and His Treasures / The Discovery of King Tut', 3: https://www.semmel-exhibitions.com/wp-content/uploads/2021/12/SC_Partnerbrochure_KingTUT_2019.pdf.

31 For Morocco, see: El-Araf, 'Replicas of King Tut's Artefacts on Display in Morocco', https://english.ahram.org.eg/NewsContent/9/40/102894/Heritage/Ancient-Egypt/Replicas-of-King-Tuts-artefacts-on-display-in-Moro.aspx. For Belgium, see: Liège University, 'Tutankhamun Exhibition in Liège', https://www.news.uliege.be/cms/c_11437116/en/tutankhamun-exhibition-in-liege.

32 The Tutankhamun Exhibition, 'The Exhibition', https://www.tutankhamun-exhibition.co.uk/the-exhibition.

33 Las Vegas Natural History Museum, 'Treasures of Egypt', https://www.lvnhm.org/exhibits?pgid=kagoho672-f0866ffc-e308-4514-8677-90697b11186b.

34 Agnew and Wong, 'Conserving and Managing the Tomb of Tutankhamen', 9–11. https://www.getty.edu/conservation/our_projects/field_projects/tut/Getty-Magazine-Tutankhamen-2019.pdf; Kenney, 'Getty Wraps Up Conservation Effort at King Tutankhamen's Tomb', https://www.theartnewspaper.com/2019/01/23/getty-wraps-up-conservation-effort-at-king-tutankhamens-tomb.

35 Factum Foundation, 'The Facsimile of Tutankhamun's Tomb: Overview', https://www.factumfoundation.org/pag/1548/the-facsimile-of-tutankhamuns-tomb-overview.

36 Factum Foundation, *The Authorized Facsimile of the Burial Chamber of Tutankhamun*, https://www.factum-arte.com/resources/files/fa/press_releases/web_tutankhamun_exhibition.pdf.

37 Reeves, *The Burial of Nefertiti?*.

38 Shaw, 'Signs Point to Two Hidden Rooms at Tutankhamun's Tomb, Experts Say', https://www.theartnewspaper.com/2015/09/29/signs-point-to-two-hidden-rooms-at-tutankhamuns-tomb-experts-say.

39 Reeves, *The Burial of Nefertiti?*, 11.

40 Shaw, 'Egypt Announces "Discovery of the Century" Hidden Behind King Tut's Tomb', https://www.theartnewspaper.com/2016/03/17/egypt-announces-discovery-of-the-century-hidden-behind-king-tuts-tomb.

41 Romey and Williams, 'Exclusive Photos: Search Resumes for Hidden Chambers in King Tut's Tomb', https://www.nationalgeographic.com/history/article/king-tut-tomb-hidden-chamber-scan-egypt.

42 Romey, 'It's Official: Tut's Tomb Has No Hidden Chambers After All', https://www.nationalgeographic.com/science/article/king-tut-tutankhamun-tomb-radar-results-science.

43 Reeves, with Ballard, *The Decorated North Wall in the Tomb of Tutankhamun (KV 62). (The Burial of Nefertiti? II)*.

44 Reeves, *The Tomb of Tutankhamun (KV 62): Supplementary Notes (The Burial of Nefertiti? III)*.

45 Shaw, 'Possible Unmapped Chambers Discovered Near Tutankhamun's Tomb', https://www.theartnewspaper.com/2019/05/09/possible-unmapped-chambers-discovered-near-tutankhamuns-tomb.

46 Tawfik, 'The Grand Egyptian Museum. Tutankhamun's New Residence', 44–48. Also see: Keyes, 'For the First Time, All 5,000 Objects Found Inside King Tut's Tomb Will Be Displayed Together', https://www.smithsonian mag.com/travel/grand-egyptian-museum-next-big-thing-180961333/.

47 El-Aref, 'In Photos: Tutankhamun Coffee Cups' Mask Replica Sets a New World Record', https://english.ahram.org.eg/NewsContent/9/40/358530/ Antiquities/Ancient-Egypt/In-Photos-Tutankhamun-coffee-cups-mask-replica-set.aspx.

48 El-Aref, 'Luxor Museum's Tut Collection Moved to Grand Egyptian Museum', https://english.ahram.org.eg/NewsContent/9/44/297398/ Antiquities/Museums/Luxor-Museums-Tut-collection-moved-to-Grand-Egypti.aspx.

49 Dawson, 'Golden Touch Up: King Tutankhamun's Coffin Undergoes First Ever Restoration at New Grand Egyptian Museum', https:// www.theartnewspaper.com/2019/08/05/golden-touch-up-king-tutankhamuns-coffin-undergoes-first-ever-restoration-at-new-grand-egyptian-museum.

50 JICA-GEM Joint Conservation Project, 'Finalizing Multispectral Imaging on Tutankhamun's Tunics', https://www.jicagem.com/blog/2020/05/ finalizing-multispectral-imaging-on-tutankhamuns-tunics/.

51   JICA-GEM Joint Conservation Project, 'Digital Microscope Analysis of King Tutankhamun's Chariots', https://www.jicagem.com/blog/2019/04/digital-microscope-analysis-of-king-tutankhamens-chariots-2/.

52   Both Tutankhamun and Ankhesenamun are named in the chariot's inscriptions. The canopy is Carter no. 123 and the chariot is Carter no. 122. See Kawai et al., 'The Ceremonial Canopied Chariot of Tutankhamun (JE61990 and JE60705): A Tentative Virtual Reconstruction'. Also see Brock, 'A Possible Chariot Canopy for Tutankhamun', 29–43.

53   Hastings, 'Tutankhamun's Last Resting Place', https://inews.co.uk/news/world/tutankhamun-last-resting-place-egypt-tourism-grand-egyptian-museum-400867.

54   El-Aref, 'Searching for the Tomb of Tutankhamun's Wife Ankhesenamun', https://english.ahram.org.eg/NewsContent/9/40/288380/Antiquities/Ancient-Egypt/Searching-for-the-tomb-of-Tutankhamuns-wife-Ankhes.aspx.

Bibliography

Agnew, Neville and Lori Wong. 'Conserving and Managing the Tomb of Tutankhamen', *The Getty* (Winter 2019), 9–11. https://www.getty.edu/conservation/our_projects/field_projects/tut/Getty-Magazine-Tutankhamen-2019.pdf.

Aldred, Cyril. 'The "New Year" Gifts to the Pharaoh', *Journal of Egyptian Archaeology* 55 (1969), 75–76.

Allen, James P. *The Art of Medicine in Ancient Egypt*, Metropolitan Museum of Art, New York, 2005.

Allen, Susan J. 'Tutankhamun's Embalming Cache Reconsidered', in *Egyptology at the Dawn of the Twenty-First Century: Proceedings of the Eighth International Congress of Egyptologists, Cairo, 2000*, vol. 1, Zahi A. Hawass and L. Pinch Brock (eds), American University in Cairo Press, Cairo, New York, 2003, 23–29.

Allon, Niv and Hana Navratilova. *Ancient Egyptian Scribes: A Cultural Exploration*, Bloomsbury Academic, London and New York, 2017.

Amarna Project. 'House of Ranefer: Background', https://www.amarnaproject.com/pages/recent_projects/excavation/house_of_ranefer/.

Amarna Project. 'Workmen's Village', https://www.amarnaproject.com/pages/amarna_the_place/workmans_village/index.shtml.

El-Aref, Nevine. 'Replicas of King Tut's Artefacts on Display in Morocco', *Ahram Online*, 4 June 2014, https://english.ahram.org.eg/NewsContent/9/40/102894/Heritage/Ancient-Egypt/Replicas-of-King-Tuts-artefacts-on-display-in-Moro.aspx.

El-Aref, Nevine. 'Tutankhamun's Gold Mask Restored After Botched Repair', *Ahram Online*, 16 December 2015, https://english.ahram.org.eg/NewsContent/9/40/173700/Antiquities/Ancient-Egypt/Tutankhamuns-gold-mask-restored-after-botched-repa.aspx.

El-Aref, Nevine. 'Searching for the Tomb of Tutankhamun's Wife Ankhesenamun', *Ahram Online*, 18 January 2018, https://english.ahram.org.eg/NewsContent/9/40/288380/Antiquities/Ancient-Egypt/Searching-for-the-tomb-of-Tutankhamuns-wife-Ankhes.aspx.

El-Aref, Nevine. 'Luxor Museum's Tut Collection Moved to Grand Egyptian Museum', *Ahram Online*, 11 April 2018, https://english.ahram.org.eg/NewsContent/9/44/297398/Antiquities/Museums/Luxor-Museums-Tut-collection-moved-to-Grand-Egypti.aspx.

El-Aref, Nevine. 'In Photos: Tutankhamun Coffee Cups' Mask Replica Sets a New World Record', *Ahram Online*, 28 December 2019, https://english.ahram.org.eg/NewsContent/9/40/358530/Antiquities/Ancient-Egypt/In-Photos-Tutankhamun-coffee-cups-mask-replica-set.aspx.

El-Aref, Nevine. 'In Photos: Tutankhamun Artefacts to Go on Display at Hurghada, Sharm Museums', *Ahram Online*, 28 August 2020, https://english.ahram.org.eg/NewsContent/9/40/378777/Antiquities/Ancient-Egypt/In-Photos-Tutankhamun-artefacts-to-go-on-display-a.aspx.

Arnold, Dorothea. *The Royal Women of Amarna: Images of Beauty from Ancient Egypt*, Metropolitan Museum of Art, New York, 1996.

Aston, Barbara G., James A. Harrell and Ian Shaw. 'Stone', in *Ancient Egyptian Materials and Technology*, Paul T. Nicholson and Ian Shaw (eds), Cambridge University Press, Cambridge, 2000, 5–77.

Austin, A.E. 'The Cost of a Commute: A Multidisciplinary Approach to Osteoarthritis in New Kingdom Egypt', *International Journal of Osteoarchaeology* 27:4 (July/August 2017), 537–550.

Baedeker, Karl. *Egypt and the Sudan: Handbook for Travellers,* seventh remodelled edition, Karl Baedeker Publisher, Leipzig, 1914.

Bell, Lanny. 'The New Kingdom "Divine" Temple: The Example of Luxor', in *Temples of Ancient Egypt*, Byron E. Shafer (ed.), Cornell University Press, New York, 1997, 127–184.

Benderitter, Thierry. 'Ay – KV 23', *Osirisnet: Tombs of Ancient Egypt*, https://www.osirisnet.net/tombes/pharaons/ay/e_ay_pharaon_01.htm.

Benderitter, Thierry. 'Ay – TA 25', *Osirisnet: Tombs of Ancient Egypt*, https://www.osirisnet.net/tombes/amarna/ay_amarna/e_ay_amarna_01.htm.

Benderitter, Thierry. 'Horemheb – Saqqara', *Osirisnet: Tombs of Ancient Egypt,* https://www.osirisnet.net/tombes/saqqara_nouvel_empire/horemheb_saqqara/e_horemheb_saqqara_01.htm.

Benderitter, Thierry. 'Huy – TT 40', *Osirisnet: Tombs of Ancient Egypt*, https://www.osirisnet.net/tombes/nobles/houy40/e_houy40_01.htm.

Benderitter, Thierry. 'Tutankhamun – KV 62', *Osirisnet: Tombs of Ancient Egypt,* https://www.osirisnet.net/tombes/pharaons/toutankhamon/e_toutankhamon_01.htm.

Biston-Moulin, Sébastien. 'Le roi Sénakht-en-Rê Ahmès de la XVIIe dynastie', *Égypte Nilotique et Méditerranéenne* 5 (2012), 61–67.

Blomstedt, Patric. 'Orthopedic Surgery in Ancient Egypt', *Acta Orthopaedica* 85:6 (2014), 670–676.

Bogensperger, Ines. 'Alum in Ancient Egypt: The Written Evidence', in *Excavating, Analysing, Reconstructing Textiles of the 1st Millennium AD from Egypt and Neighbouring Countries: Proceedings of the 9th Conference of the Research Group 'Textiles from the Nile Valley', Antwerp, 27–29 November 2015*, Antoine DeMoor, Cäcilia Fluck and Petra Linscheid (eds), Lannoo Publishers, Tielt, 2017, 255–263.

Booth, Charlotte. *Horemheb: The Forgotten Pharaoh*, Amberley, Stroud, 2009.

Brier, Bob. *Egyptomania: Our Three Thousand Year Obsession with the Land of the Pharaohs*, Palgrave Macmillan, New York, 2013.

Brock, Edwin C. 'A Possible Chariot Canopy for Tutankhamun', in *Chasing Chariots: Proceedings of the First International Chariot Conference (Cairo 2012)*, André J. Veldmeijer and Salima Ikram (eds), Sidestone Press, Leiden, 2013, 29–43.

Brorson, Stig. 'Management of Fractures of the Humerus in Ancient Egypt, Greece, and Rome. An Historical Review', *Clinical Orthopaedics and Related Research* 467 (2009), 1907–1914.

Brown, Nick. 'Tutankhamun's Sticks', American Research Center in Egypt website, https://www.arce.org/resource/tutankhamuns-sticks.

Bryce, Trevor. 'The Death of Niphururiya and Its Aftermath', *Journal of Egyptian Archaeology* 76 (1990), 97–105.

Bryce, Trevor. *Life and Society in the Hittite World*, Oxford University Press, Oxford, 2002.

Bryce, Trevor. *Letters of the Great Kings of the Ancient Near East: The Royal Correspondence of the Late Bronze Age*, Routledge, London, 2003.

Bryce, Trevor. *The Kingdom of the Hittites*, Oxford University Press, Oxford, 2005.

Bryson, Karen M. *The Reign of Horemheb. History, Historiography, and the Dawn of the Ramesside Era*, PhD diss., Johns Hopkins University, 2018.

Carter, Howard and Arthur C. Mace. *The Tomb of Tut.Ankh.Amen*, vol. 1, Cassell, London, 1923.

Carter, Howard. *The Tomb of Tut.Ankh.Amen*, vol. 2, Cassell, London, 1927.

Carter, Howard. *The Tomb of Tut.Ankh.Amen*, vol. 3, Cassell, London, 1933.

Černý, Jaroslav. *Hieratic Inscriptions from the Tomb of Tutankhamun*, Griffith Institute, Oxford, 1965.

Comelli, Daniela, Massimo D'Orazio, Luigi Folco et al., 'The Meteoritic Origin of Tutankhamun's Iron Dagger Blade', *Meteoritics & Planetary Science* 51:7 (2016), 1301–1309.

Cross, Steven W. 'The Hydrology of the Valley of the Kings', *Journal of Egyptian Archaeology* 94 (2008), 303–312.

Cross, Steven W. 'The Re-Sealing of KV62', *Ancient Egypt* 10:2 (2009), 16–22.

Crouwel, Joost. 'Studying the Six Chariots from the Tomb of Tutankhamun – An Update', in *Chasing Chariots: Proceedings of the First International Chariot Conference (Cairo 2012)*, André J. Veldmeijer and Salima Ikram (eds), Sidestone Press, Leiden, 2013, 73–93.

Cumming, Barbara. *Egyptian Historical Records of the Later Eighteenth Dynasty*, Fascicle III, Aris & Phillips, Warminster, 1984.

Darnell, John Coleman and Colleen Manassa. *Tutankhamun's Armies: Battle and Conquest During Ancient Egypt's Late 18th Dynasty*, Wiley, Hoboken, NJ, 2007.

Davies, Benedict, G. *Egyptian Historical Records of the Later Eighteenth Dynasty*, Fascicle VI, Aris & Phillips, Warminster, 1995.

Davies, Norman de Garis. *The Rock Tombs of El Amarna. The Tombs of Panehesy and Meryra II*, vol. 2, Egypt Exploration Fund, London, 1905.

Davies, Norman de Garis. *The Rock Tombs of El Amarna. The Tombs of Huya and Ahmes*, vol. 3, Egypt Exploration Fund, London, 1905.

Davies, Norman de Garis. *The Tomb of Ken-Amun at Thebes*, Metropolitan Museum of Art, New York, 1930.

Davies, W. Vivian. 'Tut'ankhamūn's Razor-Box: A Problem in Lexicography', *Journal of Egyptian Archaeology* 63 (1977), 107–111.

Davis, Theodore M. *The Tombs of Harmhabi and Touatânkhamanou*, Constable, London, 1912.

Dawson, Aimee. 'Golden Touch Up: King Tutankhamun's Coffin Undergoes First Ever Restoration at New Grand Egyptian Museum', *The Art Newspaper*, 5 August, 2019, https://www.theartnewspaper.com/2019/08/05/golden-touch-up-king-tutankhamuns-coffin-undergoes-first-ever-restoration-at-new-grand-egyptian-museum.

Depuydt, Leo. *Civil Calendar and Lunar Calendar in Ancient Egypt*, Peeters, Leuven, 1997.

Derry, Douglas E. 'Report on the Examination of Tut.Ankh.Amen's Mummy', in *The Tomb of Tut.Ankh.Amen*, vol. 2, Cassell, London, 1927, 213–232.

Desroches-Noblecourt, Christiane. *Tutankhamen. Life and Death of a Pharaoh*, The Connoisseur and Michael Joseph, London, 1963.

Digital Egypt for Universities. 'Tale of Sanehat: Two Principal Sources', University College London, 2000, https://www.ucl.ac.uk/museums-static/digitalegypt/literature/sanehat/sources.html.

Dodson, Aidan. 'The Canopic Equipment from the Serapeum of Memphis', in *Studies on Ancient Egypt in Honour of H.S. Smith*, Anthony Leahy and W.J. Tait (eds), Egypt Exploration Society, London, 1999, 59–75.

Dodson, Aidan. 'Bull Cults', in *Divine Creatures. Animal Mummies in Ancient Egypt*, Salima Ikram (ed.), American University in Cairo Press, Cairo, 2005, 72–105.

Dodson, Aidan. *The Royal Tombs of Ancient Egypt*, Pen and Sword Books, Barnsley, 2016. Ebook.

Dodson, Aidan. *Amarna Sunset: Nefertiti, Tutankhamun, Ay, Horemheb, and the Egyptian Counter-Reformation*, revised edition, American University in Cairo Press, Cairo, 2018.

Dodson, Aidan and Steven Cross. 'The Valley of the Kings in the Reign of Tutankhamun', *Egyptian Archaeology* 48 (2016), 3–8.

Dodson, Aidan and Dyan Hilton. *The Complete Royal Families of Ancient Egypt*, Thames & Hudson, London, 2004.

Eaton-Krauss, Marianne. 'Tutankhamun's Sarcophagus: An Addition and Two Corrections', *Journal of Egyptian Archaeology* 80 (1994), 217–218.

Eaton-Krauss, Marianne. *The Unknown Tutankhamun*, Bloomsbury Academic, London and New York, 2015.

Edwards, Iorwerth E.S. *Tutankhamun's Jewelry*, Metropolitan Museum of Art, New York, 1976.

Edwards, Iorwerth E.S. *Tutankhamun: His Tomb and Its Treasures*, Metropolitan Museum of Art, New York, 1976.

Epigraphic Survey, *Reliefs and Inscriptions at Luxor Temple*, vol. 1, The Festival Procession of Opet in the Colonnade Hall with Translations of Texts, Commentary, and Glossary. Oriental Institute, Chicago, 1994.

Epigraphic Survey, *Reliefs and Inscriptions at Luxor Temple*, vol. 2, The Facade, Portals, Upper Register Scenes, Columns, Marginalia, and Statuary in the Colonnade Hall, Oriental Institute, Chicago, 1998.

Factum Foundation. *The Authorized Facsimile of the Burial Chamber of Tutankhamun*, https://www.factum-arte.com/resources/files/fa/press_releases/web_tutankhamun_exhibition.pdf.

Factum Foundation. 'The Facsimile of Tutankhamun's Tomb: Overview', https://www.factumfoundation.org/pag/1548/the-facsimile-of-tutankhamuns-tomb-overview.

Fagan, Brian, M. *Lord and Pharaoh: Carnarvon and the Search for Tutankhamun*, Left Coast Press, Walnut Creek, CA, 2015.

Filer, Joyce. 'The KV 55 Body: The Facts', *Egyptian Archaeology* 17 (2000), 13–14.

Forbes, Dennis, Salima Ikram and Janice Kamrin. 'Tutankhamen's Missing Ribs', *KMT: A Modern Journal of Ancient Egypt* 18:1 (2007), 50–56.

Fryxell, Allegra. 'Tutankhamen, Egyptomania, and Temporal Enchantment in Interwar Britain', *Twentieth Century British History* 28:4 (2017), 516–542.

Fukaya, Masashi, *The Festivals of Opet, the Valley, and the New Year. Their Socio-religious Functions*, Archaeopress, Oxford, 2019.

Ghaly, Emad and Osama Ibrahim. 'Reward Ceremony Scenes in Private Tombs of Post-Amarna Period in Thebes and Memphis', *International Journal of Heritage, Tourism and Hospitality* 11:1/2 (March 2017), 170–172.

Goelet, Ogden. 'Tomb Robberies in the Valley of the Kings', in *The Oxford Handbook of the Valley of the Kings*, Richard H. Wilkinson and Kent R. Weeks (eds), Oxford University Press, Oxford, 2016, 448–466.

Griffith Institute. *Tutankhamun: Anatomy of an Excavation*, http://www.griffith.ox.ac.uk/discoveringTut/.

Guasch Jané, Maria Rosa. 'The Meaning of Wine in Egyptian Tombs: The Three Amphorae from Tutankhamun's Burial Chamber', *Antiquity* 85 (2011), 851–858.

Guasch Jané, Maria Rosa. 'About the Orientation of the Magical Bricks in Tutankhamun's Burial Chamber', *Journal of the American Research Center in Egypt* 48 (2012), 111–118.

Guasch Jané, Maria Rosa. 'Food', in *All Things Ancient Egypt: An Encyclopedia of the Ancient Egyptian World*, vol. 1, Lisa K. Sabbahy (ed.), Greenwood, an imprint of ABC-CLIO, LLC, Santa Barbara, 2019, 177–179.

Habicht, Michael E., Patrick E. Eppenberger and Frank Rühli. 'A Critical Assessment of Proposed Outbreaks of Plague and Other Epidemic Diseases in Ancient Egypt', *International Journal of Infectious Diseases* 103 (2021), 217–219.

Harer, W. Benson. 'Chariots, Horses, or Hippos: What Killed Tutankhamun?' *Minerva* 18:5 (2007), 8–10.

Harer, W. Benson. 'New Evidence for King Tutankhamen's Death: His Bizarre Embalming', *Journal of Egyptian Archaeology* 97 (2011), 228–233.

Harrell, James A. 'Violence in Earth, Water, and Sky. Geological Hazards', in *Pharaoh's Land and Beyond. Ancient Egypt and Its Neighbors*, Pearce Paul Creasman and Richard H. Wilkinson (eds), Oxford University Press, Oxford, 2017, 241–255.

Harris, J.R. 'Akhenaten and Nefernefruaten in the Tomb of Tut'ankhamūn', in *After Tut'ankhamūn: Research and Excavation in the Royal Necropolis at Thebes*, C. Nicholas Reeves (ed.), Kegan Paul International, London and New York, 1992, 55–72.

Hastings, Rob. 'Tutankhamun's Last Resting Place: Egyptians Who Rely on Tombs for Tourism Divided over Mummy's Move to the Grand Egyptian Museum', *iNews*, 22 February 2020, https://inews.co.uk/news/world/tutankhamun-last-resting-place-egypt-tourism-grand-egyptian-museum-400867.

Hawass, Zahi. *Discovering Tutankhamun. From Howard Carter to DNA*, American University in Cairo Press, Cairo, 2013.

Hawass, Zahi, Yehia Z. Gad, Somaia Ismail et al., 'Ancestry and Pathology in King Tutankhamun's Family', *JAMA: The Journal of the American Medical Association* 303:7 (2010), 638–647.

Hawass, Zahi and Sahar Saleem. *Scanning the Pharaohs: CT Imaging of the New Kingdom Royal Mummies*, American University in Cairo Press, Cairo, 2016.

Hawass, Zahi, M. Shafik, Frank J. Rühli et al., 'Computed Tomographic Evaluation of Pharaoh Tutankhamun, ca. 1300 BC', *Annales du Service des Antiquités de l'Égypte* 81 (2007), 159–174.

Hays, Harold M. 'Funerary Rituals (Pharaonic Period)', in *UCLA Encyclopedia of Egyptology*, Jacco Dieleman and Willeke Wendrich (eds), Los Angeles, January 2010. https://escholarship.org/uc/item/1r32g9zn.

Hellinckx, Bart R. 'Tutankhamun's So-called Stole', *Orientalia Lovaniensia Periodica* 27 (1996), 5–22.

Hull Museums Collections. 'The Tutankhamun Replicas at Hull Museums', 2022. http://museumcollections.hullcc.gov.uk/collections/subtheme.php?irn=4.

Ikram, Salima. 'Some Thoughts on the Mummification of King Tutankhamun', *Études et travaux* 26 (2013), 291–301.

Ikram, Salima. 'An Epistolary Footnote: Howard Carter, Saleh Hamdi Bey, and Tutankhamun's Mummy', in *Up and Down the Nile – Ägyptologische Studien für Regine Schulz. Ägypten und Altes Testament 97*, Martina Ullmann, Gabriele Pieke, Friedhelm Hoffmann and Christian Bayer (eds), Zaphon, Münster, 2021, 205–208.

Janssen, Rosalind M. and Jacobus J. Janssen. *Growing Up and Getting Old in Ancient Egypt*, Golden House Publications, London, 2007.

JICA-GEM Joint Conservation Project, 'Digital Microscope Analysis of King Tutankhamun's Chariots', 23 April 2019, https://www.jicagem.com/blog/2019/04/digital-microscope-analysis-of-king-tutankhamens-chariots-2/.

JICA-GEM Joint Conservation Project, 'Finalizing Multispectral Imaging on Tutankhamun's Tunics', 17 May 2020, https://www.jicagem.com/blog/2020/05/finalizing-multispectral-imaging-on-tutankhamuns-tunics/.

Johnson, W. Raymond. 'Honorific Figures of Amenhotep III in the Luxor Temple Colonnade Hall', in *For His Ka: Essays Offered in Memory of Klaus Baer*, David P. Silverman (ed.), Oriental Institute of the University of Chicago, Chicago, 1994, 133–144.

Johnson, W. Raymond. 'Tutankhamen-Period Battle Narratives at Luxor', *KMT: A Modern Journal of Ancient Egypt* 20:4 (2009–2010), 20–33.

Kawai, Nozomu. 'A Coronation Stela of Tutankhamun? (JdE 27076)', in *Egyptian Museum Collections around the World. Studies for the Centennial of the Egyptian Museum, Cairo*, vol. 1, Mamdouh Eldamaty and Mai Trad (eds), American University in Cairo Press, Cairo, 2002, 637–644.

Kawai, Nozomu. *Studies in the Reign of Tutankhamun*, PhD diss., Johns Hopkins University, 2005.

Kawai, Nozomu. 'Ay Versus Horemheb: The Political Situation in the Late Eighteenth Dynasty Revisited', *Journal of Egyptian History* 3:2 (2010), 261–292.

Kawai, Nozomu, Yasushi Okada, Takeshi Oishi et al., 'The Ceremonial Canopied Chariot of Tutankhamun (JE61990 and JE60705): A Tentative Virtual Reconstruction', *CIPEG Journal* 4 (2020), 1–11.

Kemp, Barry J. *Ancient Egypt: Anatomy of a Civilization*, second edition, Routledge, London, 2006.

Kemp, Barry J. *The City of Akhenaten and Nefertiti: Amarna and its People*, Thames & Hudson, London, 2012.

Kenney, Nancy. 'Getty Wraps Up Conservation Effort at King Tutankhamen's Tomb', *The Art Newspaper*, 23 January 2019, https://www.theartnewspaper.com/2019/01/23/getty-wraps-up-conservation-effort-at-king-tutankhamens-tomb.

Keyes, Allison. 'For the First Time, All 5,000 Objects Found Inside King Tut's Tomb Will Be Displayed Together', *Smithsonian Magazine*, 21 December 2016, https://www.smithsonianmag.com/travel/grand-egyptian-museum-next-big-thing-180961333/.

Kitchen, Kenneth A. *Pharaoh Triumphant. The Life and Times of Ramesses II, King of Egypt*, Aris & Phillips, Warminster, 1982.

Klemm, Rosemarie and Dietrich Klemm. *Gold and Gold Mining in Ancient Egypt and Nubia, Geoarchaeology of the Ancient Gold Mining Sites in the Egyptian and Sudanese Eastern Deserts*, Springer, Berlin, Heidelberg, 2013.

Laboury, Dimitri. 'The Artist Who Created the Most Famous Funerary Mask in the World?', in *Tutankhamun: Discovering the Forgotten Pharaoh*, Simon Connor and Dimitri Laboury (eds), Presses universitaires de Liège, Liège, 76–77.

Lacovara, Peter. *The World of Ancient Egypt: A Daily Life Encyclopedia*, Greenwood, an imprint of ABC-CLIO, LLC, Santa Barbara, 2017.

Larson, John. 'The Heb-sed Robe and the "Ceremonial Robe" of Tut'ankhamun', *Journal of Egyptian Archaeology* 67 (1981), 180–181.

Las Vegas Natural History Museum. 'Treasures of Egypt', https://www.lvnhm.org/exhibits?pgid=kagoho672-fo866ffc-e308-4514-8677-90697b11186b.

Lazaridis, Nikolaos. 'Education and Apprenticeship', *UCLA Encyclopedia of Egyptology*, Elizabeth Frood and Willeke Wendrich (eds), Los Angeles, 2010, https://escholarship.org/uc/item/1026h44g.

Leek, F. Filce. *The Human Remains from the Tomb of Tutankhamun*, Griffith Institute, Oxford, 1972.

Liège University. 'Tutankhamun Exhibition in Liège: Discovering the Forgotten Pharaoh', 14 December 2019, https://www.news.uliege.be/cms/c_11437116/en/tutankhamun-exhibition-in-liege.

Littauer, M.A. and Joost H. Crouwel. *Chariots and Related Equipment from the Tomb of Tutankhamun*, Griffith Institute, Oxford, 1985.

Lowe, Adam. 'Tomb Recording: Epigraphy, Photography, Digital Imaging, and 3D Surveys', in *The Oxford Handbook of the Valley of the Kings*, Richard H. Wilkinson and Kent R. Weeks (eds), Oxford University Press, Oxford, 2016, 528–543.

Lucas, Alfred. 'Notes on Some of the Objects from the Tomb of Tut-Ankhamun', *Annales du Service des Antiquitiés de l'Égypte* 41 (1942), 135–147.

Manniche, Lise. *Musical Instruments from the Tomb of Tutankhamun*, Griffith Institute, Oxford, 1976.

Marchant, Jo. *The Shadow King: The Bizarre Afterlife of King Tut's Mummy*, Da Capo Press, Boston, MA, 2013.

Matsui, Takafumi, Ryota Moriwaki, Eissa Zidan and Tomoko Arai. 'The Manufacture and Origin of the Tutankhamen Meteoritic Iron Dagger', *Meteoritics & Planetary Science* 57:4, (2022), 747–758.

McAlister, Melani. *Epic Encounters: Culture, Media, and U.S. Interests in the Middle East Since 1945*, University of Berkeley Press, Berkeley, Los Angeles, London, 2005.

McLeod, Wallace. *Composite Bows from the Tomb of Tutankhamun*, Griffith Institute, Oxford, 1970.

McLeod, Wallace. *Self Bows and Other Archery Tackle from the Tomb of Tutankhamun*, Griffith Institute, Oxford, 1982.

Moorey, Peter R.S. *Ancient Mesopotamian Materials and Industries: The Archaeological Evidence*, Clarendon Press, Oxford, 1994.

Murnane, William J. *The Road to Kadesh. A Historical Interpretation of the Battle Reliefs of King Sety I at Karnak*, second edition revised, Oriental Institute, Chicago, 1990.

Naunton, Chris. *Egyptologists' Notebooks*, Thames & Hudson, London, 2020.

Nomura, Kazuyo and Christina Rinaldo. *The Weavers of Tutankhamun. The Story of Recreating the Textile Treasure of a Pharaoh*, English translation by Marcus Bergman, Bokförlaget Signum, Stockholm, 2013.

Ogden, Jack, 'Metals', in *Ancient Egyptian Materials and Technology*, Paul T. Nicholson and Ian Shaw (eds), Cambridge University Press, Cambridge, 2000, 148–176.

Parkinson, Richard B. *Tutankhamun: Excavating the Archive*, Griffith Institute, Oxford, 2022.

Reeves, Nicholas. *The Complete Tutankhamun: The King, the Tomb, the Royal Treasure*, Thames & Hudson, London, 1990.

Reeves, Nicholas. *The Burial of Nefertiti?* Amarna Royal Tombs Project, University of Arizona Egyptian Expedition, Tucson, AZ, 2015.

Reeves, Nicholas. 'The Gold Mask of Ankhkheperure Neferneferuaten', *Journal of Ancient Egyptian Interconnections* 7:4 (2015), 77–79.

Reeves, Nicholas. 'Tutankhamun's Mask Reconsidered', in *Bulletin of the Egyptological Seminar* 19 (2015), 511–526.

Reeves, Nicholas. *The Tomb of Tutankhamun (KV 62): Supplementary Notes (The Burial of Nefertiti? III)*, Amarna Royal Tombs Project, University of Arizona Egyptian Expedition, Tucson, AZ, 2020.

Reeves, Nicholas, with George Ballard. *The Decorated North Wall in the Tomb of Tutankhamun (KV 62) (The Burial of Nefertiti? II)*, Amarna Royal Tombs Project, University of Arizona Egyptian Expedition, Tucson, AZ, 2019.

Reeves, Nicholas and Richard H. Wilkinson. *The Complete Valley of the Kings. Tombs and Treasures of Egypt's Greatest Pharaohs*, Thames & Hudson, London, 1996.

Reid, Donald M. 'Remembering and Forgetting Tutankhamun: Imperial and National Rhythms of Archaeology, 1922-1972', in *Histories of Egyptology: Interdisciplinary Measures*, William Carruthers (ed.), Routledge, New York, 2014, 157–173.

Riggs, Christina. *Treasured. How Tutankhamun Shaped a Century*, Atlantic Books, London, 2021.

Robins, Gay. *Women in Ancient Egypt*, British Museum Press, London, 1993.

Robins, Gay. 'The Decorative Program in the Tomb of Tutankhamun (KV 62)', in *The Archaeology and Art of Ancient Egypt. Essays in Honor of David B. O'Connor*, vol. 2, Zahi A. Hawass and Janet Richards (eds), Conseil Suprême des Antiquités de l'Égypte, Cairo, 2007, 321–342.

Robins, Gay. *The Art of Ancient Egypt*, revised edition, Harvard University Press, Cambridge, MA, 2008.

Roehrig, Catharine H. *The Eighteenth Dynasty Titles Royal Nurse (mn't nswt), Royal Tutor (mn'nswt), and Foster Brother/Sister of the Lord of the Two Lands (sn/snt mn'n nb t3wy)*, PhD diss., University of California, Berkeley, 1990.

Romer, John. *Valley of the Kings*, Michael O'Mara, London, 1981.

Romey, Kristin. 'It's Official: Tut's Tomb Has No Hidden Chambers After All', *National Geographic*, 6 May 2018, https://www.nationalgeographic. com/science/article/king-tut-tutankhamun-tomb-radar-results-science.

Romey, Kristin and A.R. Williams. 'Exclusive Photos: Search Resumes for Hidden Chambers in King Tut's Tomb', *National Geographic*, 2 February 2018, https://www.nationalgeographic.com/history/article/king-tut-tomb-hidden-chamber-scan-egypt.

Roth, Silke. 'Queen', in *UCLA Encyclopedia of Egyptology*, Elizabeth Frood and Willeke Wendrich (eds), Los Angeles, 2009, https://escholarship. org/uc/item/3416c82m.

Rühli, Frank J. and Salima Ikram. 'Purported Medical Diagnoses of Pharaoh Tutankhamun, *c.* 1325 BC-', *HOMO – Journal of Comparative Human Biology* 65 (2014), 51–63.

Säve-Söderbergh, Torgny. *Four Eighteenth Dynasty Tombs*, Griffith Institute, Oxford, 1957.

Schulze, Mario. 'Tutankhamun in West Germany, 1980–81', *Representations* 141:1 (2018), 39–58.

Semmel Exhibitions (formerly SC Exhibitions). 'Partner Brochure for Tutankhamun: His Tomb and His Treasures / The Discovery of King Tut', https://www.semmel-exhibitions.com/wp-content/uploads/2021/12/ SC_Partnerbrochure_KingTUT_2019.pdf.

Shaw, Garry J. *The Pharaoh: Life at Court and on Campaign*, Thames & Hudson, London, 2012.

Shaw, Garry J. 'Auguste Mariette, 1821–81', in *The Great Archaeologists*, Brian Fagan (ed.), Thames & Hudson, London, 2014, 56–61.

Shaw, Garry J. *The Egyptian Myths: A Guide to the Ancient Gods and Legends*, Thames & Hudson, London, 2014.

Shaw, Garry J. 'Howard Carter, 1874–1939', in *The Great Archaeologists*, Brian Fagan (ed.), Thames & Hudson, London, 2014, 100–105.

Shaw, Garry J. 'Signs Point to Two Hidden Rooms at Tutankhamun's Tomb, Experts Say', *The Art Newspaper*, 29 September 2015, https://www. theartnewspaper.com/2015/09/29/signs-point-to-two-hidden-rooms-at-tutankhamuns-tomb-experts-say.

Shaw, Garry J. 'Egypt Announces "Discovery of the Century" Hidden Behind King Tut's Tomb', *The Art Newspaper*, 17 March 2016, https://www.theartnewspaper.com/2016/03/17/egypt-announces-discovery-of-the-century-hidden-behind-king-tuts-tomb.

Shaw, Garry J. 'Steep Commute Gave Ancient Egyptian Workers Osteoarthritis', *Science*, 22 November 2016, https://www.science.org/content/article/steep-commute-gave-ancient-egyptian-workers-osteoarthritis.

Shaw, Garry J. *War and Trade with the Pharaohs. An Archaeological Study of Ancient Egypt's Foreign Relations*, Pen and Sword Archaeology, Barnsley, 2017.

Shaw, Garry J. 'Palaces', in *All Things Ancient Egypt: An Encyclopedia of the Ancient Egyptian World*, vol. 2, Lisa K. Sabbahy (ed.), Greenwood, an imprint of ABC-CLIO, LLC, Santa Barbara, 2019, 398–399.

Shaw, Garry J. 'Possible Unmapped Chambers Discovered Near Tutankhamun's Tomb', *The Art Newspaper*, 9 May 2019, https://www.theartnewspaper.com/2019/05/09/possible-unmapped-chambers-discovered-near-tutankhamuns-tomb.

Shaw, Garry J. *Egyptian Mythology: A Traveller's Guide from Aswan to Alexandria*, Thames & Hudson, London, 2021.

Simpson, William Kelly, Robert K. Ritner, Vincent A. Tobin and Edward F. Wente. *The Literature of Ancient Egypt. An Anthology of Stories, Instructions, Stelae, Autobiographies, and Poetry*, American University in Cairo Press, Cairo, 2003.

Singer, Graciela Gestoso. 'Beyond Amarna: The "Hand of Nergal" and the Plague in the Levant', *Ugarit Forschungen* 48 (2017), 223–247.

Stevens, Anna, 'Death and the City: The Cemeteries of Amarna in Their Urban Context', *Cambridge Archaeological Journal* 28:1 (2017), 103–126.

Strouhal, Eugen. *Life of the Ancient Egyptians*, Liverpool University Press, Liverpool, 1997.

Tait, W. J. *Game-boxes and Accessories from the Tomb of Tutankhamun*, Griffith Institute, Oxford, 1982.

Tawfik, Tarek Sayed. 'The Grand Egyptian Museum. Tutankhamun's New Residence', *World Heritage* 83 (2017), 44–48.

Theban Mapping Project. 'KV 55: Tiye (?) or Akhenaten (?)', https://thebanmappingproject.com/index.php/tombs/kv-55-tiye-or-akhenaten.

Theban Mapping Project. 'Tomb Digging and Cutting Techniques', 15 November 2020, https://thebanmappingproject.com/articles/tomb-digging-and-cutting-techniques.

The Tutankhamun Exhibition. 'The Exhibition', https://www.tutankhamun-exhibition.co.uk/the-exhibition.

Tyldesley, Joyce. *Egypt: How a Lost Civilization Was Rediscovered*, BBC, London, 2005.

Tyldesley, Joyce. *Nefertiti's Face: The Creation of an Icon*, Profile Books, London, 2018.

Tyldesley, Joyce. 'Tutankhamun: Who's Afraid of the Pharaoh's Curse?', *History Extra*, 9 May 2019, https://www.historyextra.com/period/ancient-egypt/howard-carter-discovery-tutankhamun-tomb-lord-carnarvon-pharaoh-curse/.

Uda, M., A. Ishizaki and M. Baba. 'Tutankhamun's Gold Mask and Throne', in *Quest for the Dreams of the Pharaohs. Studies in Honour of Sakuji Yoshimura*, Jiro Kondo (ed.), Ministry of Antiquities, Cairo, 2014, 149–177.

Van Dijk, Jacobus. 'Horemheb and the Struggle for the Throne of Tutankhamun', *Bulletin of the Australian Centre for Egyptology* 7 (1996), 29–42.

Van Dijk, Jacobus. 'The Death of Meketaten', in *Causing His Name to Live: Studies in Egyptian Epigraphy and History in Memory of William J. Murnane*, Peter Brand and Louise Cooper (eds), Brill, Leiden, 2009, 83–88.

Van der Perre, Athena. 'The Year 16 Graffito of Akhenaten in Dayr Abū Ḥinnis. A Contribution to the Study of the Later Years of Nefertiti', *Journal of Egyptian History* 7 (2014), 67–108.

Veldmeijer, André J. *Tutankhamun's Footwear. Studies of Ancient Egyptian Footwear*, Sidestone Press, Leiden, 2011.

Veldmeijer, André J. and Salima Ikram. *Chasing Chariots. Proceedings of the First International Chariot Conference (Cairo 2012)*, Sidestone Press, Leiden, 2013.

Veldmeijer, André J. and Salima Ikram. 'Tutankhamun's Sticks and Staves. The Importance of Deceptively Simple Objects', *Scribe* 5 (Spring 2020), 8–13.

Vogelsang-Eastwood, Gillian. *Pharaonic Egyptian Clothing*, Brill, Leiden, Köln, 1993.

Vogelsang-Eastwood, Gillian. *Tutankhamun's Wardrobe: Garments from the Tomb of Tutankhamun*, Barjesteh van Waalwijk van Doorn, Rotterdam, 1999.

Vogelsang-Eastwood, Gillian. 'Socks', in *Tutankhamun's Footwear. Studies of Ancient Egyptian Footwear*, André J. Veldmeijer (ed.), Sidestone Press, Leiden, 2011, 165–168.

Wilkinson, Toby. *The Rise and Fall of Ancient Egypt. The History of a Civilisation from 3000 BC to Cleopatra*, Bloomsbury, London, 2010.

Winlock, Herbert E. and Dorothea Arnold. *Tutankhamun's Funeral*, Metropolitan Museum of Art, New York, 2010.

Winstone, Harry V.F. *Howard Carter and the Discovery of the Tomb of Tutankhamun*, Constable, London, 1991.

Zivie, Alain. *La Tombe de Maïa. Mère nourricière du roi Toutânkhamon et grande du harem*, Caracara édition, Toulouse, 2009.

Zivie, Alain. 'From Maïa to Meritaten', *Saqqara Newsletter* 17 (2019), 47–60.

Index

187